Physicians Survival Guide to Litigation Stress

Understanding, Managing, and Transcending a Malpractice Crisis

Physicians Survival Guide to Litigation Stress

Understanding, Managing, and Transcending a Malpractice Crisis

by

John M. James, Ph.D., M.A., M.Div.

and

W. Edward Davis, M.D., M.B.A., M.M.M.

This book is written to provide insight into what physicians may experience as a result of litigation. The information provided is offered as food for thought. The reader is advised to check appropriate medical literature and/or consult with licensed medical, psychological, or legal professionals for personal assistance or advice on any matters related to the ideas and issues raised in this book.

We especially want to thank Scott Ott of Scott Ott Creative Inc. for his advice and efforts in the design, layout, and publishing of the book. We also greatly appreciate the assistance of Marion Stafford, Medical Editor, and Ethel Madden and Nital Sheridan along with all of the Ochsner Medical Library Staff of the Ochsner Medical Center, New Orleans. Finally, we want to thank our many friends and colleagues who gave constructive feedback on the final manuscript.

Physician Health Publications, L.L.C.
P.O. Box 356, Lafayette, CA 94549
tel: 925-283-2693
email: jjames@physicianhealthpublications.com
www.physicianhealthpublications.com

Information on bulk purchases, corporate premium sales, or academic sales can also be obtained from Physician Health Publications.

Library Of Congress Cataloging-In-Publication Data:
James, John 1946–
Physicians survival guide to litigation stress:
understanding, managing, and transcending a malpractice crisis
John M. James and W. Edward Davis
p. cm.
1. Physician – Malpractice. 2. Physician – Stress. 3. Physician – Family.
4. Physician – Psychology. 5. Physician – Well-Being.
I. Davis, W. Edward. II. Title.
cataloging number pending
ISBN: 0-9776764-0-4
SAN: 2 5 7 – 9 4 6 4

Printed in China

Who's taking care of the Caretaker

when the Caretaker's out taking care?

Table of Contents

Table of Contents

PHYSICIANS SURVIVAL GUIDE TO LITIGATION STRESS

Preface

The most frequent response I have gotten from physicians who have been sued or are undergoing litigation is that they feel an extreme sense of isolation. Not only in the legal directive to "not talk to anyone . . . not even friends" but from the stigma that being faced with a malpractice case has on us as professionals. It is for this reason that I felt I *had to* understand what malpractice *means* to physicians, assimilate the information in a way that would be helpful to others and then pass it on.

As a conscientious hard-working physician, I never thought about the possibility of my being sued. I was compulsive in my history taking, thorough in my examination of the patient and medical data, diligent in diagnosing, effective in my treatment and follow-up, and possessed what others called an excellent "bedside manner." Why would I even consider the possibility that I might be sued?

Well, it happened, and when it did, I entered a world of chaos and confusion that only seemed to deepen the further I tried to understand it. As most of us in medicine know, even the most complicated of physiological processes is actually quite easy to grasp once the facts and relationships are known. But I couldn't explain this. I wondered, How could this happen to me of all people? And why was I having the reactions I was experiencing, even though I was confident I had done nothing wrong . . . and certainly not something that others would call *"malpractice"* of all things?

My curiosity was just too great. Even when I felt I didn't know which end was up, I knew *I had to understand.* The urge to know what was going on around and within me was so great that I decided that many of the very important things in my otherwise quite happy life were going to have to be put on hold.

As a result of my mother's English teacher/perpetual student upbringing, I began my search. I did what was comfortable . . . I went back to school. Even after my training in Internal Medicine, Allergy, Immunology, and Pulmonary Medicine, and after having received an M.B.A., I still thought I needed more information. So after taking some courses through the American College of Physician Executives, I completed a Master of Medical Management degree, all the while looking for why physicians react the way they do in certain situations and under certain types of stress.

It was during this time that a friend of mine gave me a copy of John James' book, *Passion for Life.*[1] It helped me to understand the roots of my unquenchable thirst for knowledge. I also began to read everything I could get my hands on regarding physicians and their unique personalities and behavioral drivers. Much to my surprise, there was very little written on the subject. I also found myself fascinated with the neurophysiology of emotional states, thought processes, and behavioral patterns. A chance meeting and conversation with John then provided the incentive and opportunity to collaborate on this mission.

The unconditional love and support from my wife Cindy, and our children, Bren and Ellie, along with that of many friends and colleagues allowed me to dedicate this portion of my life to hopefully minimize the effects of the litigation process for other physicians and their families.

— Eddie Davis
New Orleans, Louisiana

People have a natural passion for life. This passion is the core energy that drives our lives toward positive goals. It is the vital animating force which motivates us to get more out of life, to give more back, to be more involved, and to do what's right. When this energy is expressed, we pursue goals that have personal meaning and make a positive difference in life. When this energy gets disrupted or drained, we feel frustrated and out of balance.

When Eddie and I met, we found ourselves in dialogue about how physicians under litigation stress often feel their passion for medicine wavering. Their optimism and dedication can be severely challenged. Many people define themselves by their work and commitments; this is particularly true for doctors whose lives are spent in service to others.

Having spent most of my life as a psychotherapist, educator, and consultant in health care, I understood this dedication. I know how hard physicians work to do their best, day after day, patient after patient. For most, their work is so important, and their motives for helping others are so deep. And yet, I have seen what happens when people lose their passion for life or for practicing medicine.

PREFACE

Much of my efforts have been dedicated in one way or another to "taking care of the caretaker." I have trained psychiatrists, psychotherapists, and health care professionals in the diagnosis and treatment of stress disorders, trauma and crisis counseling, and marriage and family therapy. More importantly, I have counseled physicians, their spouses and families to understand and overcome the stresses of medical practice, including the problems created by malpractice litigation.

From this I have found that there are practical strategies that sued doctors can use to understand, manage, and transcend litigation stress. When doctors are able to *understand* what they are going through, including their mental and emotional reactions, they realize how normal these reactions can be. When they understand the dynamics of their stress responses and get a sense of the bigger picture they are dealing with, they often regain their composure and focus. As they take control of their lives again and manage the confluent pressures active on them, their passion for life and medicine rebounds. They gain perspective and find ways to *manage* their personal and professional lives, even through the months or years litigation may require. Eventually the time comes when the crisis is over, the case is closed, and the legal distractions go away. On the surface, things again seem somewhat normal. At a deeper level, however, this is when physicians are able to *transcend* the experience - to stand back and see it as an unfortunate but valuable learning experience. Their lives have changed, and sometimes for the better.

With this in mind, as Eddie and I talked, we realized that we both had a passion for helping physicians under stress. This led to our working together on this project. When we started to research the medical literature, we realized there was very little practical information available that would assist doctors in understanding and overcoming the stresses of litigation. What started out as an article evolved into this book. We believed a positive approach based on solid scientific information and practical strategies was what physicians needed to manage and transcend the personal, professional, and family dilemmas a suit brings.

I hope this book will help sued physicians "get their feet back on solid ground" and regain the confidence, clarity, and productivity that was challenged by their legal ordeal. And for every physician who is helped to transcend the challenge of such a crisis, there are innumerable families, children, and patients who are also helped.

PREFACE

On a personal note, I want to thank my wife Ibis, my daughter Gabriella, and my mother Muriel, who have all offered their personal encouragement, moral support, and professional editing for this project. They have nurtured my passion for life, as I have sought to nurture the lives of others.

— John James
Lafayette, California

It is our sincerest hope that this book will be a valuable resource that physicians can immediately use to survive a legal crisis and to remain confident, healthy, and productive during the process. We also hope that it will prove to be a practical guide for those who work or live with physicians, so that they can better understand and support them during the months or years of turmoil a malpractice suit can bring. In addition, we hope that this book will be used by those who have not yet been faced with a malpractice case, so that they will be proactive and take measures to inoculate themselves before the inevitable happens.

The Impact of Litigation on Physicians

Chapter 1

In 1961, an article appeared in the *Journal of the American Medical Association* which described malpractice as being a minimal concern for doctors.[2] By 1997, there was nearly one suit for every five physicians in the United States, and that trend seems to have continued.[3] In some states and in a number of clinical specialties, this probability is one in three or even worse. In addition, a national survey by *Medical Economics* found that 58% of the nearly 1800 physicians who responded had been sued for malpractice, and more than 20% of those responding had been sued at least three times.[4,p.11]

Being sued does not mean that a physician is incompetent or inadequate. A pivotal study of 3,686 physicians concluded that "the frequency of malpractice claims increased with evidence of greater medical knowledge" and that "the most knowledgeable physicians may be sued the most."[5,p.23] This suggests that receipt of a notice of legal action does not mean that a doctor did anything wrong or is any less competent than his or her peers. Thus the sued physician is not necessarily the "bad" physician, but rather the sued physician is likely to be the traumatized physician.

In 2003 there were over 850,000 physicians in the United States,[6] yet as physician/attorney Donald Palmisano, past-president of the American Medical Association points out, "On any given day, more than 125,000 cases against physicians clog our nation's courts." This is in spite of the fact that "70 percent of those filed are closed with no payment – and physicians win 80% of the cases that do go to trial."[7] These statistics are dramatic, yet they don't adequately reflect the impact that malpractice litigation has on physicians, their families, and their practices.

Malpractice litigation or the threat of legal action can be one of the most devastating experiences a physician can face in his or her personal, professional, and family life. A malpractice suit challenges the doctor's integrity, competence, professionalism, and self-esteem. A suit denies and disclaims the doctor's best intentions and goodwill toward the patient. It implies the physician grossly misconducted his or her responsibility as a healer. It lays the blame for perceived mistreatment or an adverse outcome on the physician, and puts the doctor's well-being and reputation on the line.

When hearing of a suit, well-meaning family, friends, and colleagues may make comments they intend as good advice, such as, "Don't worry about it. It happens to a lot of doctors and I know it will turn out okay," or "Don't let it bother you. It's just the cost of doing business." Or as one dentist/attorney commented, "These things occur. They always have and always will, even to the best of us. That's why we carry liability insurance. . . . Accidents happen. Mistakes can occur. You're human; you make mistakes. You usually have insurance to cover it, just as you have automobile insurance. Accept it, and get on with your life."[8,p.23] And as a federal district judge advised, "If you are sued, don't let it bother you. . . . Let it run off your back. You must face it and deal with it, but consider it a learning experience. . . . Don't let it get to you and seek professional psychological help if you need it to cope."[9] Often statements such as these don't help. Why is that? What is it about these messages that doesn't ring true for physicians?

The psychological make-up of physicians does not allow

for such a laissez-faire attitude. Most doctors are too dedicated to their patients, their practice, and their profession to consider a suit anything less than a direct and personal assault upon their integrity, commitment, and efforts. It's not just their career that's at stake – it's their reputation, their image, and their clinical competence that are all being called into question. Therefore, when served with a malpractice suit, most physicians feel attacked, anxious, and angry.

The stress of being sued does not come and go quickly. The average case lingers on for 3 to 5 years, and is experienced like the Sword of Damocles hanging over the doctor's head. Sued physicians are frequently reminded of the case by phone calls from lawyers, requests for documents, review of briefs, depositions, etc. It becomes nearly impossible for them to forget the suit and to practice medicine as usual. Consequently, patient care suffers, the doctor's family-life becomes strained, and the physician's emotional and physical health can be affected.

This book looks at the painfully difficult experience that the majority of physicians go through when sued for medical malpractice. More importantly, it suggests options for proactive response that doctors can use to minimize the effects of litigation on their lives.

To begin, this chapter provides anecdotal stories to give an idea of what some physicians have experienced. These accounts are followed by a review of six key studies on the effects of malpractice litigation on physician behavior.

PERSONAL REACTIONS TO LITIGATION

In the *Delaware Medical Journal,* one physician explained the "no-win" position he found himself in:

> *A suit charging me with negligence was an assault upon my honor, my technical ability, my medical judgment, my self respect. Such a suit was a threat to my security. From the moment the suit was instituted, I found myself in a cannot-win, must-lose position. No matter who won the case, I was to be a loser. I was to lose sleep. I was to lose a degree of privacy which I had previously enjoyed. I was to lose reputation by accusation. I was to lose reputation yet again at the hands of inaccurate journalists. I was to lose financially for the many hours I spent away from my practice because of the time devoted to litigation.*[10,pp.93-94]

In a letter to the editor of the *American Family Physician,* another physician wrote about the emotions he went through during his litigation experience:

> *A resident and I were recently involved in a two-week trial. We experienced symptoms of paranoia such as constant feelings of being maligned, harassed and conspired against, deep resentment and inability to function. To the best of our knowledge, we had done nothing wrong, but were actually "guilty until proven innocent."* [11,p.45]

A urologist used a medical analogy to explain the trauma some physicians go through when confronted with litigation:

> *When sued, the physician is in many ways comparable to the child with enuresis because the child is convinced that he is afflicted with a shameful problem that is indeed unique and never to be discussed. In the child, this often produces personality problems and a failure mentality. There is an analogy to be drawn between enuresis and malpractice suits in that the sued physician often withdraws into himself and is less self-assured.*[12,p.184]

An allergist described the profound feeling of being naive and unprepared for the stresses of prolonged medical-legal proceedings:

> *During the litigation, your entire existence is compromised by thoughts of the potential ramifications to your medical practice, to your professional reputation, to your personal relationships with friends and family, and to your financial security. You will actually progress, at varying times, through stages of disbelief, anger, depression, and eventually some form of acceptance, stages not unlike those faced by patients with a newly diagnosed and potentially terminal illness.*[13,pp.403-404]

The challenge of a lawsuit to one's personal and professional self-esteem can be so great that there seems to be no way out. In the *Journal of the Medical Association of Georgia* a brief but poignant comment is found:

> *On Tuesday, November 25, 1986, a family practitioner felt so keenly dishonored and degraded by what he saw happening to himself that he killed himself. Nothing*

ambiguous, nothing vague, and absolutely and undeniably vivid. A man who was sensitive and intelligent is dead.[14,p.116]

STUDIES OF PHYSICIANS' REACTIONS TO LITIGATION

Studies have been conducted since 1984 to determine what specific patterns of emotional and behavioral response are found among physicians when they are sued for malpractice. They confirm what many doctors have personally observed – that anxiety, anger, and/or depression often arise in response to litigation stress, and that these feelings can lead competent, dedicated doctors to become tense and uptight, distracted, cynical, or severely distressed. As a result, some doctors start to practice "defensive medicine" while others lose interest in their practice altogether. Some turn to alcohol or drugs for relief, while a few feel so overwhelmed they become suicidal.

The following presents a review of six key studies which have been done in the United States and an analysis of the response patterns they noted in order to highlight what one might expect to go through if sued.

1984 Study of Sued Physicians

The seminal study of physicians' reactions to malpractice litigation was done by Sara Charles, a psychiatrist at the University of Illinois, along with other colleagues from Loyola University in Chicago. Charles began her research after her own struggle with a malpractice suit.[15] In this first study done in 1984, 154 physicians who had been sued for malpractice were surveyed. Results indicated that 87.9% of the physicians acknowledged feeling anger, 74.3% experienced feeling "inner tension," and 71.9% admitted to having "depressive moods" in response to legal action.[16]

More notable is the fact that two primary clusters of clinically significant stress reactions to being sued were reported – depression and anger. Of the physicians surveyed, 39.1% acknowledged experiencing symptoms of a major depressive disorder such as feelings of being defeated, feelings of worthlessness, indecision, decreased appetite, and decreased sex drive, while 20.3% reported experiencing pervasive anger symptoms, such as inner tension, frustration, irritability, insomnia, fatigue, gastrointestinal symptoms, or headaches.

In addition, Charles' survey also found that 8.1%

complained of the onset of physical illness and 7.4% acknowledged exacerbation of a previously diagnosed illness; 2.9% indicated they were involved in excessive alcohol or drug use, and at the extreme, 2.2% admitted to having suicidal thoughts. Only 4.2% reported no physical or emotional symptoms associated with the malpractice suit.

Noteworthy is that almost all of the physicians surveyed (89.6%) considered their suits to be unjustified, and the majority (60.4%) considered settling of their cases would represent an admission of guilt. As a consequence of the litigation experience, 61.8% of the doctors began to practice more "defensive medicine" by ordering more diagnostic tests, while 41.8% stopped seeing certain kinds of patients, and 28.2% stopped performing specific high-risk procedures. As a consequence of the legal ordeal, 33.6% even considered retiring early.

In addition to these professional consequences, more than half of the sued physicians (56.6%) felt they and their families had suffered from the litigation experience. In discussing the results, Charles and her associates noted that physicians tended to keep their thoughts and feelings about the litigation experience to themselves; suppression and silence were "typical coping mechanisms" for sued physicians. Only about 10% sought moral support from their peers.

1985 Study of Sued vs. Non-Sued Physicians

In 1985, Charles and associates conducted a second survey of 355 physicians.[17] This study went one step further than the 1984 study in that the researchers surveyed physicians who had been sued and compared their responses to physicians who had never been sued. Sued physicians were more likely to stop seeing patients with whom the risk of litigation seemed great (48.9% vs. 29.5%). Sued physicians were also more likely to think about retiring early (42.9% vs. 30.3%). And sued physicians were more likely to discourage their children from pursuing medicine as a career (32.0% vs. 19.0%). These differences suggest a significant disenchantment with the practice of medicine as a consequence of being sued. This study also corroborated the fact that over 95% of physicians reported significant physical or emotional reactions to being sued.

From the data of the 1984 and 1985 surveys, Charles drew a number of conclusions. The word used spontaneously and almost invariably to describe the overall experience of being sued was "devastated." The most common initial reaction to being sued was anger, but over time the most enduring reaction patterns were anger *and* depression. Other ways that doctors responded to being sued included anxiety, denial, fear, guilt, and shame. Charles and associates concluded that "the majority of physicians reported an initial period of distress and, in some cases, an extended time of emotional disequilibrium with varying degrees of somatic dysfunctions."[18,p.174]

1987 Study of Sued vs. Non-Sued Physicians

In 1987, Charles and associates did a third survey in which they again compared the experience of sued to nonsued physicians.[19] Of 80 physicians who were interviewed, 51 had been sued and 29 had not. The results of these interviews indicated patterns that were similar to those of the previous surveys, with 60% of sued physicians acknowledging at least a temporary period of angry and/or depressive reactions to the experience of being sued.

Several additional findings stood out, however, when compared to the previous studies. Nearly one in five physicians mentioned the onset or exacerbation of a physical illness due to the litigation experience. As a way of dealing with their feelings, 8% of the sued physicians in this study admitted to alcohol abuse whereas 10% reported seeking psychological therapy to help them through the crisis. In addition, over 88% of the total sample (including both sued and nonsued physicians) believed that the climate of litigation had a negative influence on the quality of their relationships with patients and 75% made consequent changes in the way they practice. Possibly more significant is the fact that almost 1 out of every 4 of the sued physicians (23%) considered their litigation experience as being the most stressful period of their lives.

1988 Study of Physicians on Trial

A fourth study in 1988 by Charles and associates surveyed 64 physicians who had gone all the way to trial for a malpractice suit.[20] As this survey was of physicians who actually went to court rather than settle their cases beforehand, some significant results were found. As might be expected, 97% of the physicians reported having some emotional and/or physical reactions to going to court: 86% acknowledged feelings of inner tension, while 80% noted a depressed mood, and 70% reported anger reactions. A significant finding of this study was that 70% of those surveyed reported having talked about their litigation stress with one of their peers, as compared to only 10% of those reporting in the 1984 study.

1988 Study of Physicians' Appraisal of the Impact of Litigation on Their Lives

In another study in 1988 by Charles and associates, 50 doctors who had been sued for medical malpractice were surveyed.[21] They were clustered into two groups: those who considered a malpractice suit to have been the most stressful event in their lives (22%), and those who considered the litigation experience to not have been their most stressful event (78%).

Physicians who reported their malpractice suit to be the most stressful event of their life considered it so for one of three reasons: "the plaintiff was either a personal friend or a patient of long standing; the suit generated feelings of low self-esteem, humiliation, or self-doubts about their competence (stimulated in some instances by wide media attention); or the suit resulted in overwhelming feelings of anger, frustration, and devastation – often expressed as feeling betrayed by the 'system.'"[21, p.150] In this group, none of the doctors had been divorced or suffered the death of a spouse or child.

The second group was made up of physicians who felt that the legal crisis was not the most stressful event in their lives. They considered events such as divorce, family illness, the death of a family member, or a life-threatening illness to have been more stressful than malpractice litigation.

Physicians who experienced litigation as the worst experience in their lives had developed significantly more physical and emotional symptomatology. They experienced more insomnia, loss of interest in usual activities, gastrointestinal symptoms, and had more tension, difficulty concentrating, frustration, irritability, and social withdrawal. They reported significantly greater symptoms of major depressive disorders and pervasive anger. Professionally, they were more likely to stop performing high-risk procedures and to order more diagnostic tests for their own protection.

On the other hand, physicians who did not consider their litigation experience to be the worst event of their lives referred to the stress they associated with the suit more in terms of the time it consumed and its nuisance value. These physicians were coping more effectively with the litigation stress, and were more likely to believe they had performed competently and correctly in the patient situation in question.

From this study, Charles and associates concluded that having to cope with other major stressful events in the past puts the litigation experience into a less frightening perspective and "inoculates" the doctor against the full impact of new stressors.

1991 Study of Physicians' Stress Response Patterns

Building upon Charles' studies, Catherine Martin and associates from the Departments of Psychiatry and Behavioral Science at the University of Kentucky reported a study in 1991 of 234 doctors to determine physicians' psychological reactions to malpractice litigation stress.[22] The survey respondents were divided into three groups: 1) those who had never been sued, 2) those who had been sued within the past 2 years, and 3) those who had been sued more than 2 years before the study.

The results of this study present a different perspective of this issue than that presented by Charles' previous studies. Martin and associates identified four distinct stress response patterns by sued physicians. These included 1) a "psychologic trauma" cluster, 2) a "shame/doubt" cluster, 3) a "job strain" cluster, and 4) an "active coping" cluster.

The Psychologic Trauma Cluster

trauma =	physicians "had recurrent intrusive recollections and nightmares, withdrew from others or interests, became upset when around symbols of the event, had ruminations about the event."
anxiety =	physicians experienced "palpitations, anxiety, and were shaky, jumpy, restless, and tense."
depression =	physicians reported "decreased appetite, change in sleep, low energy, less enjoyment, and self-doubt."
anger =	physicians reported feeling "bitterness, lack of cheerfulness, indignation, hurt; feeling of being used and having life interrupted."

The Shame/Doubt Cluster

physicians reported symptoms of “discouragement, contamination, shame, fear, self-doubt, mind going blank, being overwhelmed, needing to explain to others what happened.”

The Job Strain Cluster

physicians reported “practicing defensive medicine, feeling on guard, fears of losing everything, loss of enjoyment in work, disdain for the legal system, feeling that medicine has become litigious.”

The Active Coping Cluster

physicians were taking a proactive stance in dealing with tension rather than ignoring or denying the need for addressing the crisis. Involved in this cluster was an attitude of “wanting to make some good come from the experience, wanting to fight back, planning how to deal with the problem in the future.”

As one might expect, the results of the survey by Martin and associates reinforced the conclusion that "malpractice litigation affects the physician's psychologic well-being, practice behavior, and view of medicine."[22,p.1304] This study went further, however, to suggest that the psychological reactions of sued physicians are "similar to reactions of other trauma victims."[22,p.1304] This conclusion is supported by the fact that 53% of those respondents who had been sued within 2 years of the survey reported experiencing symptoms of psychological trauma, including intrusive thoughts and compulsive rumination, tension and restlessness, sleep disturbance and fatigue, and other problematic physical and mental reactions. Furthermore, these symptoms continued to persist for 33% of those doctors whose suit occurred more than 2 years previous to the study. In addition, those physicians who had been sued more than once reported significantly greater psychological trauma symptoms than did physicians who had been sued only once. The authors suggest that this "may be due to the physician's continuous reexposure to situations that could lead to repeated malpractice litigation and further trauma."[22,p.1303]

Physicians experienced feelings of shame and doubt within the first 2 years of being sued, but after that time such feelings seemed to dissipate and return to normal levels.

The level of job strain caused by a malpractice suit was of particular significance. Of the recently sued physicians, 80% reported experiencing high levels of job strain, as compared to 42% of the doctors who had not been sued. This represents a dramatic increase in the number of physicians who felt the pressures of work to be great, and supports the conclusion that malpractice litigation creates serious challenges to a physician's medical practice. This study also found that job strain remained high for 64% of those doctors who had been sued more than 2 years previous to the survey.

Table 1

Highlights of "Physicians' Psychologic Reactions to Malpractice Litigation" [22, p.1302]

	Never sued	Sued within 2 years of the study	Sued more than 2 years prior to the study
• Psychologic trauma	13%	53%	33%
• Shame and doubt	7%	18%	5%
• Job strain	42%	80%	64%

Martin and associates suggest that sued doctors who "can see litigation as a job hazard and not an indictment of their ability as physicians . . . will be better able to mobilize adaptive coping mechanisms such as improved office practices and active participation in their defense and to minimize negative coping such as self-blame."[22,p.1303]

Martin and associates conclude their study by noting that malpractice is an unavoidable aspect of the practice of medicine nowadays, and that "physicians should be knowledgeable about the symptoms and time course of the psychologic reaction to the allegation of malpractice so that they can recognize that what they are going through is ***normal.***"[22,p.1304]

The Physician's Personality

Chapter 2

To understand how doctors respond to the crisis of being sued, it is useful to consider typical personality characteristics which predispose them to act as they do.

In 1982 a survey by Adam Krakowski of 100 randomly selected physicians, a significant finding was made: "All declared themselves to be 'compulsive personalities.'"[23,p.14] Commenting on this study in a later *JAMA* article entitled "The Role of Compulsiveness in the Normal Physician," Menninger Foundation psychiatrist Glen Gabbard suggested that what is considered *normal* in a physician – meaning the behavioral characteristics that are seen in the majority of physicians – is compulsiveness. Non-compulsive physicians are considered the oddity.[24]

Data regarding personality traits of students accepted into medical school also concur with this finding. In a study reported by Nancy Stilwell et al. in 2000, information collected on 3,987 individuals from 12 medical schools indicated a clear preference for the "judging" temperament, which they defined as dealing with the world in a planned, organized way.[25] These are traits that reflect compulsiveness. Furthermore, Mollie Wallick and Karl Cambre indicated that in their reviews of similar studies, there has been an increasing trend toward selecting physicians who demonstrate this characteristic.[26,p.380] This emphasis on medical students being selected for their compulsive tendencies was corroborated by Jock Murray, physician director of a medical humanities program, who remarked, "We want people who are driven, who are competitive, who can excel at everything that they do. What do they do when they get into practice? They try to do everything, and they have this complex which also says they must succeed at everything."[27,p.145]

Medical school is just the start. Residency training further reinforces compulsive behaviors. In his article on compulsiveness, Gabbard notes:

> *Whatever preexisting personality type may be attracted to the field of medicine, most would agree that the process of medical education itself enhances and positively reinforces whatever preexisting compulsiveness is present. There is some evidence that the premedical curriculum, the medical school experience, and the stresses of residency foster the development of certain defense mechanisms that are typical of compulsive personalities.*[24,p.2927]

This same conclusion is made about physicians who have been practicing for many years. As a result of her many studies of physicians, Charles concludes that "as a group, doctors tend to possess common personality features which render them vulnerable to such an attack. Their obsessive-compulsive personality traits stimulate them to be careful, conscientious, and prepared to consider alternative diagnostic possibilities or explore other treatment options."[28,p.171] Thus the practice of medicine demands some compulsivity, and those attracted to the field are likely people who have these traits to begin with.

COMPULSIVITY IS NORMAL

Medicine is different from most other professions in that it deals with human health and can have life-or-death consequences. Not only do patients demand excellence of their doctors, physicians demand it of themselves. There is no room for error. It is not acceptable to ignore an abnormal lab result, to miss a diagnosis, to misread an x-ray, or to miscalculate a dose of medication. The medical profession demands the utmost of care and concern in dealing with human lives and health. Therefore, a much higher dose of compulsivity is required in physicians than in many other professions.

When the word *compulsive* is used, it sometimes carries negative connotations, such as when it is used to refer to someone who is preoccupied with being perfect, demands to have things done their way, and has to be in control of their surroundings and other people. This negative usage of the term implies someone who is excessive and obsessive, someone who is driven to do something or just can't let go. This connotation of the word "compulsiveness" is not what is intended here. From a positive perspective, compulsiveness can be defined as the strong urge, drive, or conviction to achieve desired results.

The studies and articles by Krakowski[23] and Gabbard[24] were based on a definition of compulsive personality disorder found in the *Diagnostic and Statistical Manual of Mental Disorders (DSM-III)* which presents essentially a pathology model. The conceptual assumption underlying the DSM-III is that compulsivity is a problem when taken to the extreme or when the major purpose of the activity is lost or that a specific behavior interferes with completing the task, or is excessive and interferes with normal routines and occupational, academic, or social relationships.[29,pp.326-328]

Juxtaposed to this point of view, compulsivity can be understood as a normal behavior when expressed in moderate amounts or appropriate settings. Everyone has some compulsiveness in them. For example, there is a compulsiveness in people who collect things, whether they collect antiques, art, or baseball cards. There is a compulsiveness that people exhibit in their scheduling their day to get to their meetings or taxiing children around. Raising a family, paying bills, doing car maintenance, or repairing a house all require some careful and thoughtful planning and follow-through.

Leaders also have compulsive character traits. To succeed, they need to be responsible, to take charge, to work hard, to make judicious decisions, to be both wise and practical, and to make order out of chaos. Thus compulsiveness is often found in corporate executives and professionals, such as lawyers, architects, and accountants as well as doctors, dentists, and nurses.

So the popular perception that compulsiveness is always pathological is a misconception. Compulsiveness is dysfunctional only when it is taken to extremes that cause long-term problems to one's career or social relations. Otherwise, compulsive behaviors are normal and can be beneficial in a wide range of situations.

This chapter looks at the positive and negative aspects of compulsiveness as they influence physician behavior.

CHARACTERISTICS OF HEALTHY COMPULSIVITY

Five principle characteristics of positive compulsiveness found in most normal physicians are:

- Responsible and preferring to be in control
- Conscientious and striving for excellence
- Curious and independent thinking
- Practical and pragmatic
- Dedicated to productivity and positive outcomes

Each will be briefly considered.

1. Responsible and Preferring to Be in Control

By the very nature of the profession, doctors have to be responsible. Their diagnoses, treatments, clinical or surgical interventions, education, advice, and case management all have to be based on sound judgment. As captains of the ship, they supervise the actions of others and are not only clinically but also legally responsible for the performance of nurses and other health care professionals. Physicians are held answerable for tough decisions, even when they're made quickly with less-than-complete information or in the midst of a life-or-death emergency. It is this sense of responsibility and willingness to be in control that Sir William Osler describes in *Aequanimitas* when he writes of doctors having a "coolness and presence of mind under all circumstances, calmness amid storm, clearness of judgment in moments of grave peril."[30,p.4]

2. Conscientious and Striving for Excellence

Patients expect their doctors to be perfect, and physicians have that same expectation of themselves. To attain this level of performance, physicians have to be conscientious. They need to be on the alert for possible adverse drug interactions. They need to be diligent in pursing the unusual diagnosis, and willing to take the time to research an uncommon presenting symptom or disease process, even though it is done on uncompensated time. It is this conscientiousness that motivates physicians to "go the extra mile" and to check and re-check laboratory results for discrepancies or inconsistencies. Physicians must also adhere to strict codes of ethics and standards of care. In order to do so, they must operate in a planned and organized manner. This tendency of conscientiousness also extends to other aspects of practice, such as returning patients' phone calls, making sure their pagers work when on call, explaining things in ways their patients can understand, and arranging to meet with patients' families to discuss medical conditions when appropriate. As one family practitioner explained, "You rarely get sued for doing too much. You get nailed for doing too little."[31,p.239]

3. Curious and Independent Thinking

A third characteristic which reflects the compulsiveness in most physicians is that of judicious and independent thinking. Physicians need to be discerning in their observations and self-reliant in their medical interpretations and decisions. Eager to acquire information or knowledge, curious physicians may search and investigate, ponder, and imagine what's going on beneath the surface of a medical enigma. They may stay late into the night following a hunch or researching an intuitive suspicion. Or they may study collateral fields of medicine or explore less academic pursuits such as music and the arts, food and wine, sports, gardening, or travel. Physicians are just naturally curious people.

4. Practical and Pragmatic

Physicians have to be practical and pragmatic. They need to make sensible decisions that are efficacious and cost effective. They need to take into consideration the risk-benefit ratio when they prescribe medications or recommend any medical or surgical interventions. Physicians also have to be realistic and willing to accept unknown and uncontrollable variables that affect patients and their outcomes. They understand that medicine is an art as well as a science, and that they have to work with the foibles and imperfections of medical knowledge and health care systems. Doctors send patients to hospitals for surgery and other treatments when they know there is a chance of an iatrogenic complication. They realize that medicine entails some risk and that both patients and themselves often have to live with some unknowns and factors beyond their control.

5. Dedicated to Productivity and Positive Outcomes

Physicians are dedicated to maintaining and improving health. The primary concern of physicians and patients is the clinical outcome. A positive outcome is how physicians are graded, how they know they did their job well. A lot of personal satisfaction comes with a good outcome, and anxiety and concern when there is an adverse one. But physicians are realistic and know that they can't always produce the results their patients want. Some processes can't be stopped; some diseases can't be healed. So while physicians do their best to achieve positive outcomes, they also have to be realistic and willing to deal with less than ideal results.

Medical practice also requires that physicians be goal driven, yet willing to set priorities and change them as circumstances demand. In a busy emergency department, the physician in charge has to triage sick patients according to the available medical and staff resources. In a clinic, goal and priority setting is also necessary when the physician has four patients waiting in treatment rooms, a nurse needing clinical direction, a pharmacist asking for a phone-in prescription, and the physician's spouse holding on the phone to talk about their own sick child. While directing their attention to many problems at once and keeping their priorities straight, physicians also know that at any moment they may have to shift their priorities due to another phone call, page, or emergent situation.

THE DARK SIDE OF COMPULSIVITY

While compulsive traits in physicians allow them to perform well in their profession, those same traits can also lead to less than ideal behaviors and consequences. As the Committee on Medical Liability of the American Academy of Pediatrics explains:

> *Physicians obsessive-compulsive personality traits are very helpful to the physician and patient. They stimulate physicians to be careful, responsible, conscientious, and prepared to consider a wide range of diagnostic possibilities and treatment options. Physicians also tend to have high expectations of themselves and are consequently self-critical.*
>
> *When a physician is sued, however, these same personality traits generate self-doubt, self-scrutiny, feelings of guilt and shame, and often self-condemnation. Often the event that generated the suit already has been a source of sleepless nights and self-accusations, even in instances in which the physician performed with the highest level of competence. To be legally accused of*

negligence for such an event is enormously disturbing. [32:pp.188-189]

Gabbard adds that the maladaptive ways over-compulsivity impacts the physician include "difficulty in relaxing, reluctance to take vacations from work, problems in allocating time to family, an inappropriate and excessive sense of responsibility for things beyond one's control, chronic feelings of 'not doing enough,' difficulty setting limits, hypertrophied guilt feelings that interfere with the healthy pursuit of pleasure, and the confusion of selfishness with healthy self-interest."[24,p.2926]

This tendency toward "over-compulsivity" leads to some significant observations. In his survey of physicians, Krakowski found that 20% described themselves as being so intense that they possessed 4 of the 5 behaviors associated with "compulsive personality disorder" as defined by the *Diagnostic and Statistical Manual of Mental Disorders [DSM-III].* Eighty percent of the respondents exhibited 3 of the 5 diagnostic behaviors.[23,p.21] This means that during "normal conditions," most physicians exhibit many of the diagnostic criteria for a diagnosis of Compulsive Personality Disorder. The DSM-IV revision expanded this diagnosis to include eight traits and renamed it the "Obsessive-Compulsive Personality Disorder."[33,pp.672-673]

Table 2

Key Diagnostic Criteria for Obsessive-Compulsive Personality Disorder [33,p.729]

A pervasive pattern of preoccupation with orderliness, perfectionism, and mental and interpersonal control, at the expense of flexibility, openness, and efficiency, beginning by early adulthood and present in a variety of contexts, as indicated by four (or more) of the following:

1. Is preoccupied with details, rules, lists, order, organization, or schedules to the extent that the major point of the activity is lost.

2. Shows perfectionism that interferes with task completion (e.g., is unable to complete a project because his or her own overly strict standards are not met).

3. Is excessively devoted to work and productivity to the exclusion of leisure activities and friendships (not accounted for by obvious economic necessity).

4. Is overly conscientious, scrupulous, and inflexible about matters of morality, ethics, or values (not accounted for by cultural or religious identification).

5. Is unable to discard worn-out or worthless objects even when they have no sentimental value.

6. Is reluctant to delegate tasks or to work with others unless they submit to exactly his or her way of doing things.

7. Adopts a miserly spending style toward both self and others; money is viewed as something to be hoarded for future catastrophes.

8. Shows rigidity and stubbornness.

Physicians' Reactions to Litigation

Chapter 3

"A physician's identity is often tightly bound up with his or her work, so a suit is perceived as a personal attack" and a professional insult, notes Thomas Hobbs, medical director of a physician's health program in Pennsylvania.[34,p.22] The sense of being attacked ignites a range of reactions, the most common being anger, depression, and anxiety. This chapter considers how each of these behavioral responses can be expressed and understood.

ANGRY RESPONSES TO LITIGATION

My deposition went well, but the trial judge was pushing for a settlement. Just before the scheduled trial, my attorney advised me to settle. The jurors weren't likely to understand the medical issues involved, he explained. Instead, they would probably decide the case on an emotional basis: whether I was more likable than Mrs. Warren, and how sorry they felt for her when they saw her in a wheelchair.

My attorney argued that the risks of going to trial clearly outweighed the benefits. If I went to trial, I might win. But if I lost, I'd risk a verdict that might exceed my coverage. If I settled the case, however, it would be over.

I felt violated. No matter how much venom I spewed about the faults of our malpractice system, the poison stayed within me. Who else would sue me now, I wondered? What if the next patient has an adverse effect from a medication I prescribed? What if the patient has an unfortunate outcome despite proper care?

My rage at plaintiff's lawyers and the legal system went on unabated. Ultimately, I needed counseling to help me get through it. Only now, nearly two years later, am I finally ridding myself of the poison.[35]

Anger is a common response reported by physicians confronted by legal action. The following briefly considers the diagnostic criteria for anger responses as pertains to doctors under litigation stress.

Malpractice litigation may lead to a low-level anger which is expressed as impatience, tenseness, or irritability. Feeling this way, doctors may act abrupt with phone calls, be curt and uncaring with patients, or get easily frustrated when things take longer than expected.

As litigation pressures build, physicians tend to become less resilient to the demands of the profession and normal tasks may become burdensome. Anger may be expressed as being unsympathetic or even cynical toward patients, acting annoyed and defensive with patient complaints, or being impatient with children, the elderly, or the infirm. Increased tensions may also lead to snapping at staff, barking orders, getting angry at having to do unscheduled procedures, being critical and negative about anything having to do with the practice, acting impatient and quick tempered while driving, quarreling with family members, or acting obnoxious or argumentative with most everyone. And at the extreme, physicians under litigation stress may slip into moments of hostility or even rage, throwing files or instruments, yelling at nurses or receptionists, even walking out on scheduled appointments or the practice altogether.

Clinically, anger can be understood as both an internal feeling and an external behavior. Internally, anger often arises from the belief that one has been treated unfairly or trespassed upon in some way. Feeling unjustly accused as many doctors do when sued, they may feel annoyed, irritated, and unsettled. This is often accompanied by racing thoughts and difficulty concentrating. Associated physiological symptoms can include increased heart rate, rapid breathing, agitation and hyperarousal, and tension in the jaw, shoulders, or stomach.

In a 2004 survey of over 1600 members of the American College of Physician Executives, more than 95% reported encountering these disruptive behaviors "on a regular basis." These behaviors included "browbeating nurses and pharmacists, dressing down hapless staff, belittling patients to their faces, swearing at the tops of their voices, muttering ominous threats, dripping sarcasm and snide innuendo, slouching in late day after day, raging, sulking, hurling surgical instruments, blowing off appointments, sabotaging meetings, sneering at administrators, insulting their colleagues, . . ."[36,p.6] The Institute for Safe Medication Practices reported similar results in a 2003 survey of over 2000 pharmacists, nurses, and other hospital workers.[37]

While some doctors may be expressive and vent their anger on people or things, others may be more restrained and show little external emotion, even though they are experiencing considerable internal turmoil and stress. Some show their anger by complaining about life, medicine, insurance reimbursements, etc., while others try to suppress their anger and act as if nothing's wrong, while their internal tension surfaces in headaches, gastrointestinal distress, or other physical ailments.

As anger builds, it begins to show in external behaviors that may range from rudeness, sarcasm, derogatory statements, or accusatory remarks, to cursing, yelling, slamming things, and aggressive personal attacks.

Within the medical world, the phrase "disruptive physician" is often used to describe doctors who exhibit significant or chronic anger. For example, the American Medical Association defines disruptive behavior as "a style of interaction with physicians, hospital personnel, patients, family members, or others that interferes with patient care."[38] Purposefully, this definition is both broad and vague, allowing for a wide range of behaviors and consequences to be included.

Many state medical societies have policies that are more explicit regarding the behaviors they consider disruptive. The staff policies of the Medical Center of the University of California at Irvine, for example, identify three classifications of disruptive behavior based on their level of severity.[39] Level 1 refers to "physical violence or other physical abuse which is directed at other people." Level 2 refers to "verbal abuse such as unwarranted yelling, swearing, or cursing; threatening, humiliating, sexual or otherwise inappropriate comments directed at a person or persons; or physical violence or abuse directed in anger at an inanimate object." Level 3 refers to "verbal abuse that is directed at-large, but has been reasonably perceived by a witness to be disruptive behavior." These policy definitions highlight the range of dysfunction that can be encountered among physicians.

Lynn Hankes, Director of the Washington Physicians Health Program, provides a list of even more specific symptomatic behaviors exhibited by disruptive physicians, including "inappropriate anger or resentments; intimidation; abusive language; blames or shames others for possible adverse outcomes; unnecessary sarcasm or cynicism; threats of violence, retribution, or litigation."[40] Hankes also targets other disruptive behavior such as "uncooperative, defiant approach to problems; rigid, inflexible responses to requests; sexual harassment, comments or innuendoes; seductive, aggressive, or assaultive behavior; racial, ethnic, or socioeconomic slurs" as well as a general "lack of regard for personal comfort and dignity of others."[40] The Arkansas Hospitals Association adds that chronically angry physicians often rationalize aberrant behavior, manipulate and misrepresent information or events, deal in power, and do not respond appropriately to emergency or night calls.[41]

The consequences of such attitudes and behavior for the doctor can be devastating. A joy for life and for medical practice can decline, as can one's personal health and well-being. Patients may not come back, colleagues may stay away, and/or major family problems or divorce can ensue. The following is how one medical consultant explained the dilemma:

> *It used to be that abused staff tended to stay and take abuse. Today staff not only leave, they hire employment attorneys and file hostile-work-environment lawsuits. Partners of the disruptive physician often worry about being named in lawsuits because they did not have a policy to confront the situation. . . . Staff working with the physician often lose confidence and self-esteem. They routinely turn their stress against other staff, themselves (increased sickness), patients (decreased courtesy), and the physician. . . . It is no wonder that turnover in a*

> *practice with a disruptive physician is inordinately high and expensive.*[42]

Administratively, additional consequences arise in response to the angry, disruptive physician:

> *Staff frequently hold back information or try to decrease communication and contact. Other physicians in the practice may feel obligated to correct or cover up for the disruptive physician. . . . Administrators waste time protecting their staff from the physician, increase their time counseling disgruntled patients and spend an inordinate amount of time dealing with the demands of the disruptive individual. Hospital administrators often feel trapped because of their medical staff's fear of the angry, intimidating, perhaps litigious physician.*[42]

All this highlights the seriousness of the impact an angry physician can have on patients, employees, and the practice, not to mention on the family as well as him or herself.

DEPRESSIVE REACTIONS TO LITIGATION

Physicians who are usually upbeat and productive can go through a serious depressive reaction to a malpractice suit. The reaction can come quickly, be fairly intense, then diminish as the doctor reestablishes psychological equilibrium, or the reaction can become part of the physician's daily mood and last for years.

Depression – either brief or chronic – is a common reaction to the long and trying experience of a legal defense. Depositions and the discovery process drag on. Months of wondering and being caught off guard by unexpected phone calls and legal maneuvers add to the stress of waiting for a final decision. Add to this the demeaning personal and professional impact of litigation or court appearances and it is easy to understand why so many sued physicians feel deeply discouraged, depressed, and sometimes even suicidal.

Depression that arises from a legal action can be deep and express itself in many forms. For example, doctors feeling their integrity is being called into question may start to lose interest in their practice. They may start taking longer lunch hours and seeing fewer patients. They may come into work tired and leave exhausted. They may avoid returning phone calls and lock themselves in their office when not needed in the examining or operating room. They may avoid other doctors and conveniently miss going to conferences and CME programs. Their expressions may become glum and their responses to patients and staff more mechanical than real.

During those times when the pressures increase, depression may increase and more overt symptoms occur. Disturbance of sleep patterns and feelings of guilt or self-doubt may lead to a generalized disengagement from family or friends. At the office, avoidance of paperwork and indecision with office management issues may become frequent. There may even be unwanted moments when the doctor becomes tearful or looks as if he or she has been crying.

When the pressure seems too great, there may be thoughts or talk of quitting the practice, or at the extreme of committing suicide. These thoughts may be momentary and pass quickly, or they may linger and become clinically significant.

Like anger, depression has internal psychological and physiological reactions as well as external behavioral expressions. As Charles noted in her studies of sued physicians, depressed doctors tend to feel guilt and shame, helpless, hopeless, worthless, and defeated. Physiologically depressed doctors reported experiencing sleep disturbances (especially insomnia), fatigue, and a general slowing of motor activity. This was often accompanied by a decreased appetite and sex drive. Externally, physician depression is characterized by changes in mood, lack of interpersonal vitality, and professional and social withdrawal.

Symptoms of a depressive reaction may surface briefly at the first sign of a lawsuit and then dissipate within a short time, or they may ebb and flow over the course of years that the suit takes to be finally resolved. When an initial reaction arises but then recedes within a few weeks to 6 months, the physician may be experiencing an adjustment reaction or disorder to the stress of being sued. If the symptoms of the physician's stress reactions are more pervasive and have a more significant impact on work performance, then the doctor is more likely going through an episode of a major depressive disorder.

The predominant symptoms of a depressive Adjustment Disorder are depressed mood, tearfulness, or feelings of hopelessness. Symptoms may also include a wide range of additional behaviors. For example, doctors experiencing a depressed adjustment disorder may act moody, lethargic, unmotivated, or show little spontaneity or interpersonal warmth. And yet, in spite of these symptoms, they may handle their practice fairly well and many of their normal personality traits and behaviors may still come through in their interactions with patients, colleagues, and staff.

Table 3

Key Diagnostic Criteria for Adjustment Disorder with Depressed Mood [33,p.683]

A. The development of emotional or behavioral symptoms in response to an identifiable stressor(s) occurring within 3 months of the onset of the stressor(s).

B. These symptoms or behaviors are clinically significant as evidenced by either of the following:

1. Marked distress that is in excess of what would be expected from exposure to the stressor.

2. Significant impairment in social or occupational (academic) functioning.

C. The symptoms do not represent bereavement.

D. Once the stressor (or its consequences) has terminated, the symptoms do not persist for more than an additional 6 months.

A depressive episode or disorder is more severe than a temporary adjustment disorder. A depressive episode is manifested by intense feelings of failure, worthlessness, or excessive and inappropriate guilt that go beyond self-evaluation and self-reproach.[33,pp.320-327] Thoughts of being helpless and powerless to change things may lead the person to feeling hopeless and defeated. Normal activities and professional relationships may begin to seem meaningless. A sense of resignation and apathy may set in. Further, a brooding preoccupation with the suit may lead to memory difficulties, distractability, indecisiveness, and problems thinking clearly or concentrating for extended periods of time. Furthermore, the person may have a tendency to deny, discount, or explain away any or all of these symptoms, while secretly entertaining recurrent thoughts of self-harm or suicidal ideation.

These psychological symptoms are often accompanied by physiological symptoms that the doctor seems unable to control. The person may exhibit serious fatigue, lethargy, and loss of energy, or a psychomotor agitation that exceeds mere restlessness. In a depressive episode, normal body rhythms are often disturbed. Significant weight changes can occur, sleep disturbances are common, and a disinterest in sex may develop.

Table 4

Key Diagnostic Criteria for Major Depressive Episode [33,p.356]

A. Five (or more) of the following symptoms have been present during the same 2-week period and represent a change from previous functioning; at least one of the symptoms is either (1) depressed mood or (2) loss of interest or pleasure.

1. Depressed mood most of the day, nearly every day, as indicated either by subjective report (e.g., feels sad or empty) or observation made by others (e.g., appears tearful).

2. Markedly diminished interest or pleasure in all, or almost all, activities most of the day, nearly every day (as indicated by either subjective account or observation made by others).

3. Significant weight loss when not dieting or weight gain (e.g., a change of more than 5% of body weight in a month), or decrease or increase in appetite nearly every day.

4. Insomnia or hypersomnia nearly every day.

5. Psychomotor agitation or retardation nearly every day (observable by others, not merely subjective feelings of restlessness or being slowed down).

6. Fatigue or loss of energy nearly every day.

7. Feelings of worthlessness or excessive or inappropriate guilt ... nearly every day (not merely self-reproach or guilt about being sick).

8. Diminished ability to think or concentrate, or indecisiveness, nearly every day (either by subjective account or as observed by others).

9. Recurrent thoughts of death, recurrent suicidal ideation without a specific plan, or a suicide attempt or a specific plan for committing suicide.

Table 4 *[continued]*

B. The symptoms do not meet criteria for a Mixed Episode.

C. The symptoms cause clinically significant distress or impairment in social, occupational, or other important areas of functioning.

D. The symptoms are not due to the direct physiological effects of a substance (e.g., a drug of abuse, a medication) or a general medical condition (e.g., hypothyroidism).

E. The symptoms are not better accounted for by bereavement, i.e., after the loss of a loved one, the symptoms persist for longer than 2 months or are characterized by marked functional impairment, morbid preoccupation with worthlessness, suicidal ideation, psychotic symptoms, or psychomotor retardation.

Doctors are often reluctant to seek help when they are feeling seriously depressed. They are used to helping others but resist seeking medical help for themselves, especially when they are dealing with an emotion-based condition. In a recent clinical review article on the depressed physician, authors Ruth Levine and Stephen Bryant note that "despite widespread attempts to destigmatize depression and psychiatric treatment, many continue to view depression as a weakness or character flaw rather than an involuntary and blameless medical illness."[43,p72] Hesitance to seek help goes beyond personal attitudes and hesitance. Physicians may not seek treatment because of professional and institutional barriers as well. "The problem has been that boards or bodies that issue privileges at hospitals and health plans have been asking diagnosis-related questions that assume professional impairment if a physician declares a diagnosis."[44]

This becomes a double bind, because a depressive disorder is not the same as a passing blue mood, nor is it a sign of personal weakness or a condition that can be wished or willed away. People with a depressive illness cannot merely "pull themselves together" and get better. Without treatment, symptoms can last for a long time and the consequences can add up. To avoid the potential for self-medicating, appropriate treatment is important when the depression begins to affect one's clinical practice.

ANXIETY IN RESPONSE TO LITIGATION

Anxiety is the third reaction physicians most often experience when sued. Anxiety is a very uncomfortable feeling to contend with as it is hard to control or to deal with effectively. At its core, anxiety is an apprehensive feeling about the future; an expectation that things will go wrong or get worse.

It is hard for anyone facing a lawsuit not to worry about a negative outcome, due to the potential for an adverse legal decision resulting from a judge's or jury's bias, the threat of the public finding out about the accusations, or the possibility of peers losing respect and treating the sued doctor like a pariah. Understandably it is hard *not* to worry, much less not stress out.

Anxiety in physicians is expressed in a variety of ways. Some doctors get nervous and fidgety, unable to sit still long enough to read a professional journal, much less read a book, while others get worried and preoccupied when not with patients. Some become indecisive and self-doubting, whereas others feel so fearful they have panic attacks. In an attempt to maintain control over their emotions and reactions, some doctors become hyper-intense and over-controlling. There are many ways anxiety can eat away at people when they feel attacked.

In the psychiatric literature, there are a dozen different diagnostic categories which fall under the heading of "anxiety disorders" and numerous others in which anxiety is an essential feature. Three diagnostic patterns which pertain to doctors confronted with a medical malpractice suit are Adjustment Disorder with Anxiety, Generalized Anxiety Disorder, and Acute Stress Disorder.

Adjustment Disorder with Anxiety refers to a condition in which a wide range of anxiety symptoms may be possible, but worry, nervousness, and jitteriness are the predominant reactions noted.[33,pp.624-627] Characteristic of this diagnosis is that the symptoms arise in response to a stressor of any severity, whether mild or extreme.

The onset of symptoms occurs within 3 months of an identifiable stressor. Thus the experience and expression of a rather continuous anxiety might develop soon after a patient implies or directly threatens litigation, even when there appears to be no just cause. Symptoms may also develop after the occurrence of a significant and potentially litigious adverse medical event, or after a series of problematic medical cases.

Symptoms of worry, nervousness, and agitation may be present for anywhere from a few weeks to months, and can lead to decreased performance at work or significant changes in family or social relationships. However, a primary characteristic of this diagnosis is that anxiety symptoms dissipate within 6 months of the termination of the stressor or its negative consequences.

As the symptoms appear in reaction to an identifiable stressor of any severity, a diagnosis of Adjustment Disorder with Anxiety could pertain to the physician who becomes worried about being sued after an adverse encounter with a patient, or to a physician who experiences mild yet continuous anxiety in response to a malpractice suit.

Table 5

Key Diagnostic Criteria for Adjustment Disorder with Anxiety [33,p.683]

A. The development of emotional or behavioral symptoms in response to an identifiable stressor(s) occurring within 3 months of the onset of the stressor(s).

B. These symptoms or behaviors are clinically significant as evidenced by either of the following:

1. Marked distress that is in excess of what would be expected from exposure to the stressor.

2. Significant impairment in social or occupational functioning.

C. The stress-related disturbance does not meet the criteria for another specific disorder and is not merely an exacerbation of a preexisting disorder.

D. The symptoms do not represent bereavement.

E. Once the stressor (or its consequences) has terminated, the symptoms do not persist for more than an additional 6 months.

Generalized Anxiety Disorder refers to a condition of worry and apprehensive expectation that are present much of the time.[33,pp.432-435] Anxious feelings tend to hover around in one's psyche, making it nearly impossible to relax and think clearly. This agitated emotional state is difficult for the person to control, which only makes things worse.

The symptoms of generalized anxiety may include being easily distracted and having difficulty concentrating. Irritability, muscle tension, restlessness, inability to relax, gastrointestinal discomfort, sleep disturbance, and both physical and emotional fatigue are other symptoms. This disorder may also lead to fidgeting, tension headaches, trembling, continuous nervousness, lightheadedness, sweating, palpitations, tachycardia, dizziness, or dry mouth.[45] Constant anxiety naturally affects people's attitudes toward everyday, routine life circumstances and leads to significant distress in personal, professional, and social arenas of life. For this diagnosis to apply, symptoms must be present for at least 6 months.

The following are the diagnostic criteria for Generalized Anxiety Disorder.

Table 6

Key Diagnostic Criteria for Generalized Anxiety Disorder [33,p.476]

A. Excessive anxiety and worry (apprehensive expectation), occurring more days than not for at least 6 months, about a number of events or activities (such as work or school performance).

B. The person finds it difficult to control the worry.

C. The anxiety and worry are associated with three (or more) of the following six symptoms (with at least some symptoms present for more days than not for the past 6 months).

1. Restlessness or feeling keyed up or on edge.
2. Being easily fatigued.
3. Difficulty concentrating or mind going blank.
4. Irritability.
5. Muscle tension.
6. Sleep disturbance (difficulty falling or staying asleep, or restless unsatisfying sleep).

D. The anxiety, worry, or physical symptoms cause clinically significant distress or impairment in social, occupational, or other important areas of functioning.

In spite of the fact that at first glance many doctors under stress would seem to be exhibiting signs and symptoms of a Generalized Anxiety Disorder, it is more likely that they are suffering from an Acute Stress Disorder or perhaps even Post-Traumatic Stress Disorder. This is because diagnostically, Generalized Anxiety Disorder is a condition without precipitants and the intensity, duration, or frequency of the anxiety and worry is far out of proportion to the actual likelihood or impact of the feared event.[33,p.432-436] Due to the specific precipitant of legal action a doctor faces and the potential seriousness of its consequences, a physician's high anxiety could be considered appropriate to the situation and thus the diagnosis of Generalized Anxiety Disorder would likely not apply.

More serious and also more appropo to the experience of physicians sued for medical malpractice are two disorders that are similar in many ways except for their duration: Acute Stress Disorder and Post-Traumatic Stress Disorder.

Acute Stress Disorder refers to a cluster of anxiety symptoms resulting from exposure to a traumatic event or events in which the person "experienced, witnessed, or was confronted with" an event that involved 1) the actual or threatened death or serious injury to oneself or others, or 2) a threat to the physical integrity of oneself or others. The experience needs to have been personally significant enough that the person responded with intense fear, helplessness, or horror.[33,pp.429-432]

People suffering from Acute Stress Disorder often experience an initial sense of shock and disbelief to the sentinel event. This state gradually gives way to a heightened sense of physiological and emotional arousal or nervous agitation. Intrusive thoughts and feelings – ranging from flashbacks and repetitive memories to nightmares and anxiety – accompany and complicate their internal turmoil. Furthermore, these invasive thoughts and uncontrollable feelings are so disconcerting that a virtual "retraumatization" is believed to occur. Frequently such traumatized individuals try to avoid situations or stimuli that act as reminders of the original traumatic event. This often leads to a significant degree of numbing, detachment, avoidance, or other dissociative responses.

In the weeks that follow a stressful event, traumatized individuals often want to talk to someone about their experience, but hold back out of fear that the conversations could spark even further anxiety. And yet the memories and all the feelings and thoughts associated with them keep recycling through their awareness and keep bobbing to the surface, often when they are least expected.

Luckily, over time, most people are able to begin to understand their experience or at least accept the painful reality of what occurred. They are able to make the necessary changes in their worldview and beliefs. They "come to terms" with what they experienced. Within a few weeks, they feel less fearful and more able to return to normalcy in their lives.

When considering physicians under stress, witnessing life-threatening events is not uncommon for most doctors, especially during their training and residency. They learn to emotionally distance or dissociate themselves from the medical crisis in order to perform necessary interventions. And yet, even for seasoned physicians, there are occasionally patients whose negative outcomes seem to matter more. The doctors suffer along with those patients through unexpected catastrophes, intense pain, and drawn-out illnesses. Something about those patients make their cases more poignant and their agonies more personally touching. But then with the rush of other patients and the interactions with other colleagues and staff, somehow time passes and the doctors' attention returns to more routine cases. This seems to be part of the normal life cycle of many doctors.

But when experiencing or witnessing a serious injury or death of a patient, and then on top of that to be accused of causing the problem, it is not surprising that many doctors are thrown into a personal and professional upheaval.

Many doctors respond with shock and dismay when they learn they've been sued. After the initial reaction wears off, however, feelings ranging from mild distraction to intense fear often develop. In an effort to keep these unwanted feelings in control, doctors try to stay calm, act normal, and keep up a good front. Underneath the professional facade, however, they may be worrying incessantly. Being compulsive and conscientious, doctors served with a complaint are likely to go over and over again in their heads the events and results in question, cross-examining themselves at every step, looking for some way in which they may have been negligent or caused harm. As days pass, they are often unable to avoid the distasteful memories of being served notice and begin to worry about the adversarial climate of depositions, or the embarrassment of going to trial and being made to look bad. Feelings of anxiety build and become hard, if not impossible, to control.

Sued physicians often find themselves thinking about the case, the adverse event, the legal notice, or other related things when they should be paying attention to their patients, their paper work, or their families. They often experience flashbacks to specific events and get exhausted from fearful dreams at night. Second guessing themselves or imagining the worst possible legal or professional outcome, they tend to experience symptoms of restlessness, inability to concentrate, gastrointestinal discomfort, irritability, etc.

All of this may lead to high anxiety and restlessness in which it becomes hard to concentrate and take the necessary time to complete reports or other business tasks. Doctors in this condition may become hypervigilant with patients, afraid that the least untoward comment or medical discomfort may spark another suit. Continuing to practice using approaches or procedures that have been called to question can only make things worse. In addition, working with colleagues or staff who were involved in the adverse events, or interacting with people who simply know about it, may be so awkward and humiliating that anxiety about the situation may grow like weeds untended in a garden. All of this can lead to so much discomfort that sued physicians begin to feel disconnected, as if they were in a dream or a movie yet being outside observers watching themselves. Or it can lead to feelings of depersonalization, where doctors feel as if their personal existence has little value so they begin to function like automatons just going through the motions. As a consequence, anxious doctors also tend to withdraw from people or activities they feel can be avoided so they can deal with their anxiety in private.

Table 7

Key Diagnostic Criteria for Acute Stress Disorder [33,p.471]

A. The person has been exposed to a traumatic event in which both of the following were present:

1. The person experienced, witnessed, or was confronted with an event or events that involved actual or threatened death or serious injury, or a threat to the physical integrity of self or others;

2. The person's response involved intense fear, helplessness, or horror.

B. Either while experiencing or after experiencing the distressing event, the individual has three (or more) of the following dissociative symptoms:

1. A subjective sense of numbing, detachment, or absence of emotional responsiveness.

2. A reduction in awareness of his or her surroundings (e.g., "being in a daze").

3. Derealization.

4. Depersonalization.

5. Dissociative amnesia (i.e., inability to recall an important aspect of the trauma).

C. The traumatic event is persistently reexperienced in at least one of the following ways: recurrent images, thoughts, dreams, illusions, flashback episodes, or a sense of reliving the experience; or distress on exposure to reminders of the traumatic event.

D. Marked avoidance of stimuli that arouse recollections of the trauma (e.g., thoughts, feelings, conversations, activities, places, people).

E. Marked symptoms of anxiety or increased arousal (e.g., difficulty sleeping, irritability, poor concentration, hypervigilance, exaggerated startle response, motor restlessness).

Table 7 *[continued]*

F. The disturbance causes clinically significant distress or impairment in social, occupational, or other important areas of functioning or impairs the individual's ability to pursue some necessary task, such as obtaining necessary assistance or mobilizing personal resources by telling family members about the traumatic experience.

G. The disturbance lasts for a minimum of 2 days and a maximum of 4 weeks and occurs within 4 weeks of the traumatic event.

This diagnosis of Acute Stress Disorder is not without limits, however, when applied to physicians being sued for medical malpractice. Pathologic symptomatology arising from the adverse medical event may not be triggered or manifest until the doctor is notified or served with a lawsuit, which may occur much later than 1 month after the original traumatic event. At that time, the physician may be flooded with feelings and behavioral reactions that had been lying dormant. This would mean, however, that the doctor's condition would fall outside of the diagnostic timeline set for Acute Stress Disorder.

A second factor is that it is unlikely that the anxiety symptoms which arose in response to the crisis would subside within a month. With all the legal conversations, briefs, depositions, challenges, and responses serving as unavoidable reminders of the traumatic medical and legal events, diminution of symptoms is unlikely. In fact, just the opposite is more probable; the symptoms will probably continue on almost unavoidably for an extended period of time. Even for doctors who seek pharmacological support and psychotherapy early, unpredictable reminders of the trauma and its ensuing crisis and the uncontrollable symptoms that had surfaced are likely to exacerbate the condition again and again.

Consequently, it is more likely that a diagnosis of post-traumatic stress disorder is appropriate. Although PTSD is technically classified as an anxiety disorder, anger and depressive symptoms are often manifest with severe anxiety reactions. Therefore, for the purpose of this book, PTSD is being especially highlighted because of its apparent prevalence among sued physicians.

POST-TRAUMATIC STRESS DISORDER

To this point, no one diagnosis reviewed has adequately explained the ebbs and flows of a physician's emotions when sued. The diagnosis of Post-Traumatic Stress Disorder (commonly referred to as "PTSD") may be more appropo as the symptoms last longer than 1 month, are difficult to control, and can be personally, socially, and occupationally devastating.

The primary criteria for diagnosis of PTSD are based on both 1) a traumatic experience(s) and 2) the person's reaction to that experience.[33,pp.424-429] Like Acute Stress Disorder, the basic diagnostic criterion for PTSD is that the person must have experienced, witnessed, or been confronted by an event(s) that involved actual or threatened death or serious injury, or a threat to the physical integrity of oneself or others. This may include learning about the unexpected or violent death, serious harm, or threat of death or injury experienced by a family member, loved one, or other close friend or associate. Furthermore, the event needs to have been so disturbing that the person responded with feelings of intense fear, helplessness, or horror.

PTSD is known to result from a variety of major stressors, such as experiencing a natural event (e.g., a tornado or flood), a man-made disaster (e.g., a drowning or car accident), a violent assault, the death of a loved one, being raped or sexually abused, being in military combat, surviving torture or a terrorist attack, or other similar experiences.

PTSD may also arise from *causing* the death or severe

harm to another, according to Bonnie Green, of the Traumatic Stress Study Center at the University of Cincinnati School of Medicine.[46] Sometimes people inadvertently cause harm to another, such as in an unavoidable car accident. Other people have societally sanctioned jobs in which someone might be harmed, such as police apprehending violent criminals, fire fighters dealing with innocent victims, or physicians handling patients who have adverse medical outcomes.

PTSD is generally characterized by three primary conditions:

Hyperarousal, such as nervousness, agitation, hypervigilance, difficulty concentrating, irritability, and sleep problems

Intrusive thoughts, such as flashbacks, dreams, recurrent thoughts and memories

Emotional numbing or avoidance of reminders of the trauma, accompanied by detachment and diminished interest in normal activities, and estrangement from others

A key feature of PTSD is that intrusive thoughts and memories of the precipitating experience continue to be replayed. Nightmares, even hallucinations may be experienced. Elements of the crisis cannot be forgotten. Flashbacks are often the most distressing symptom for the PTSD sufferer. He or she experiences the traumatic experience as if it is happening in the present moment rather than at some time in the past. There is a momentary loss of time and place and the event seems to be happening "now." The traumatic event is not merely being remembered, it is being psychologically relived again and again. This causes the person to remain psychologically and even physiologically "embedded in the trauma as a contemporary experience, instead of being able to accept it as something belonging to the past."[47,p.9]

Added to this, the person feels upset by exposure to cues or symbolic reminders of the traumatic event and gradually develops a selective attention and aversion to such stimuli which becomes increasingly more inclusive and generalized.[47,p.10] As James McGaugh of the Department of Psychobiology at the University of California at Irvine explains:

> *You form a memory for the event. Each time you think about that event, rehearse it in your memory, the same emotional reaction is experienced again. In addition, the same hormones that etched that memory are released again. The next day you have another flashback and another inadvertent, unplanned rehearsal of the stressful experience. Each rehearsal of that experience, and the accompanying hormonal release, causes that memory to grow stronger. Left unchecked, this overremembrance leads to nightmares and more flashbacks. Eventually the disorder takes over your life.*[48,p.127]

Not only is there a frequent and fearful reliving of the past, there is also a severe anxiety about the future and the possibility of a repeat experience. Naturally the person does not want to experience a similar trauma again, but knows that the future cannot be controlled and the potential for a similar trauma exists. In addition, the traumatized individual is afraid of the overwhelming emotional disequilibrium and chaos that are being experienced and could worsen if the trauma is repeated.

All of these thoughts, memories and their concomitant bodily sensations become so distressful that they create in the person a near-continuous state of hyperarousal. Emotionally and physically, persons suffering from PTSD often develop a hypervigilance and exaggerated startle response. They may feel restless and agitated, and have difficulty concentrating or completing tasks. They may also have difficulty falling or staying asleep.

Bessel van der Kolk, Professor of Psychiatry at Boston University and one of the primary researchers in the field, explains some of the problems that such hyperarousal can create: "People with PTSD tend to move immediately from stimulus to response without often realizing what makes them so upset. They tend to experience intense negative emotions (fear, anxiety, anger, and panic) in response to even minor stimuli." Van der Kolk suggests that this continuous alert condition causes people "to experience sleep problems, both because they are unable to quiet themselves sufficiently to go to sleep, and because they deliberately wake themselves up in order to avoid having traumatic nightmares."[47,p.13] This heightened arousal can become so problematic that it can lead to symptoms that approximate full-fledged panic attacks.

Such intrusive thoughts and hyperarousal are so difficult to endure that persons with PTSD attempt to "shut down" or become numb to the intrusive thoughts and cues. To do so, the person may avoid activities, places, or people that arouse recollections of the traumatic experience, or they forget significant aspects of the event altogether. They may feel detached or estranged from other people, and develop a markedly restricted range of affect and ability to deal with interpersonal emotions, especially those associated with intimacy, tenderness, and sexuality. They may further develop a sense of anxiety or despair about the future and a diminished interest in significant or pleasurable activities in the present. In other words, traumatized individuals emotionally numb or anesthetize themselves to the world and other people.

The consequences of "shutting down" are of great import. Van der Kolk explains:

> *In an apparent attempt to compensate for their chronic hyperarousal, traumatized people seem to shut down: on a behavioral level, by avoiding stimuli that remind them of the trauma; on a psychobiological level, by emotional numbing, which extends to both trauma-related and everyday experiences. Over time, people with chronic PTSD come to suffer from numbing of responsiveness to*

> *the environment, punctuated by intermittent hyperarousal in response to emotionally arousing stimuli. Thus, they come to suffer both from generalized hyperarousal and from physiological emergency reactions to specific reminders. . . . This makes them either overreact and intimidate others, or to shut down and freeze. . . . The price for shutting down is decreased involvement in ordinary, everyday life.*[49,pp.S50-S51, S58]

This triad of symptoms – intrusive thoughts, hyperarousal, emotional dissociation and numbing – are not the only indicators of PTSD.[50] Additional feelings and behaviors associated with PTSD also include feelings of ineffectiveness, shame, or despair. People with PTSD may complain of loss of previously cherished beliefs, personality characteristics, or even essential aspects of self-identity. They may even feel permanently damaged and thus helpless to turn things around for the better. Or they may experience a loss of meaning in their life or activities. At the same time, they may exhibit hostility towards others and manifest impulsive or self-destructive behavior. Thus, PTSD is a condition that leaves people acting severely distressed and feeling helpless much of the time.

Table 8

Key Diagnostic Criteria for Post-Traumatic Stress Disorder [33,p.467]

A. The person has been exposed to a traumatic event in which both of the following were present:

1. The person experienced an event that involved actual or threatened death or serious injury, or other threat to one's physical integrity; or witnessed an event that involves death, injury, or a threat to the physical integrity of another person; or learned about the unexpected or violent death, serious harm, or threat of death or injury experienced by a family member or other close associate.

2. The person's response involved intense fear, helplessness, or horror.

B. The traumatic event is persistently reexperienced in one (or more) of the following ways:

1. Recurrent and intrusive distressing recollections of the event, including images, thoughts, or perceptions.

2. Recurrent distressing dreams of the event during which the event can be replayed or otherwise represented.

3. Acting or feeling as if the traumatic event were recurring (includes a sense of reliving the experience, illusions, hallucinations, and dissociative flashback episodes, including those that occur on awakening or when intoxicated).

4. Intense psychological distress at exposure to internal or external cues or triggering events that symbolize or resemble an aspect of the traumatic event.

5. Physiological reactivity on exposure to internal or external cues or triggering events that symbolize or resemble an aspect of the traumatic event.

Table 8 *[continued]*

C. Persistent avoidance of stimuli associated with the trauma and numbing of general responsiveness (not present before the trauma), as indicated by three (or more) of the following:

1. Efforts to avoid thoughts, feelings, or conversations associated with the traumatic event.

2. Efforts to avoid activities, places, or people that arouse recollections of the traumatic event.

3. Dissociative amnesia or inability to recall an important aspect of the trauma.

4. Diminished responsiveness to the external world (referred to as "psychic numbing" or "emotional anesthesia"); diminished interest or participation in significant activities.

5. Feeling detached or estranged from other people.

6. Markedly reduced or restricted range of affect and ability to feel emotions (especially those associated with intimacy, tenderness, and sexuality).

7. Sense of a foreshortened future (e.g., does not expect to have a career, marriage, children, or a normal life span).

D. Persistent symptoms of increased arousal (not present before the trauma), as indicated by two (or more) of the following:

1. Difficulty falling or staying asleep.

2. Irritability or outbursts of anger.

3. Difficulty concentrating or completing tasks.

4. Hypervigilance.

5. Exaggerated startle response.

E. Duration of the disturbance (symptoms in Criteria B, C, and D) is more than 1 month.

F. The disturbance causes clinically significant distress or impairment in social, occupational, or other important areas of functioning.

Although most people, including doctors, would not like to think of themselves as suffering from PTSD, in fact many physicians who are sued go through an extended period of severe anxiety reactions resulting from this condition. Not only do physicians experience their part in the trauma of the patient who experienced a real or perceived adverse event, sued doctors also experience the legal accusation as an assault on their personal and professional integrity and livelihood. Intense shock, fear, and panic can be experienced when served with a subpoena or notice to appear at a deposition or court hearing.

Once a malpractice attorney has been contacted, the emotional effects of the suit are made worse by directives that don't allow the physician to discuss any element of the case with anyone other than the defense attorney, who may be unwilling or unable to deal with the emotional turmoil the case creates for the physician.

Limited by the injunction to remain silent, the physician is often left alone reviewing the event or case in the privacy and isolation of his or her own mind, while experiencing a range of distressing feelings associated with them. Physicians often obsess about elements of the case or its defense, and doggedly search for aspects or information that may have been overlooked, misrepresented, or misinterpreted.

In their hyper-attention to the case and its defense, physicians may become listless and preoccupied with their dilemma and less attentive and involved with others. Consequently they may seem or act less emotionally attached, responsive, or caring towards others. Their fear of an adverse outcome may overshadow their enjoyment of normal personal or professional activities and relationships.

Often the pain and anxiety experienced by sued physicians is so great that they avoid situations in which the allegation occurred, such as not performing certain procedures or not seeing certain types of patients. Even going to work can become anxiety provoking. Doctors facing a lawsuit often withdraw socially and professionally, not spending time with colleagues or attending medical meetings out of fear of being questioned or embarrassed.

As a consequence of all this inner tension, physicians facing a legal assault may become hypervigilant out of the fear of making a mistake or being accused of one. They may also have difficulty concentrating on the business or relationships at hand because of being preoccupied with their own personal crisis.

They may have difficulty falling asleep, or staying asleep, and find themselves thinking about the case in night's dark hours. And with all this tension, they may become irritable and have outbursts of anger that are uncalled for or overly intense. Making things even a bit more confusing, these symptomatic behaviors may rise and fall in intensity or duration over the length of the case as legal demands or personal pressures ebb and flow.

The Neurophysiology of PTSD

Chapter 4

In order to appreciate what it is like for doctors to experience PTSD, it is useful to understand the many levels at which the effects of the condition are experienced. Besides the behavioral, emotional, cognitive, interpersonal, and social levels PTSD typically affects, sued physicians are also affected at neuroanatomical, neuroendochrinologic, neurochemical, and cellular levels.

This chapter is intended for doctors and others who have a background in physiology and want to understand what's going on in the body that causes such severe cognitive, emotional, and/or behavioral reactions to chronic stress. However, this chapter may be far too technical for many readers, or it may provide much more information about neurophysiology than you want or need. If that's the case, you might prefer to skim the chapter briefly, or skip it entirely and go on to the next chapter. If however, you are interested in understanding trauma physiology, this chapter may be worth your time.

The brain is a complex network of interrelated structures that function in such a way that leads to appropriate perception, understanding, and behavior. However, under certain conditions this well-regulated and integrated system experiences stimulus overloads which lead to system "short circuits" and pathologic states. Among them are the "inability to mobilize an adequate response, inability to achieve normal recovery, and inability to calibrate the magnitude of the stress response to the actual psychobiological demands of the traumatic situation."[51,p.428]

In order to understand what physiologically causes such behavior in physicians under litigation stress, it is useful to review the basic structures and processes of the brain, then to consider how these structures and their interwoven systems malfunction when trauma or prolonged stress is experienced.

The primary systems affecting persons experiencing PTSD include 1) the limbic system; 2) neurochemical systems; 3) the neocortical system; and 4) the immune system. These systems are not separate entities but rather are interactive networks with multiple functions and feedback loops. For clarity of understanding their relation to PTSD, a simplified review of these systems follows.

1. THE LIMBIC SYSTEM

The limbic system is a cluster of structures situated in the center of the brain surrounded and protected by the frontal, parietal, temporal, and occipital lobes. Most stimuli coming from the body's sense receptors pass through limbic structures on their way to the brain for processing and response.

The limbic system's most fundamental functions are to maintain a physiological and psychological balance between internal experience and external reality. Limbic structures also serve an array of functions, from self-preservation and procreation to memory management and emotional regulation.[52,pp.214-216] For example, under normal conditions the limbic system generates and modulates primal emotions such as anger, fear, and anxiety, and interweaves these emotional impulses "with higher thoughts and perceptions to produce a broad, flexible repertoire of highly complex emotional states" such as peace, joy, disgust, frustration, envy, surprise, and delight.[53,p.42]

The primary structures of the limbic system are the thalamus, amygdala, hippocampus, hypothalamus, and the corpus callosum. There are a number of associated subcortical nuclei such as the parahippocampus, the limbic midbrain, the cingulate gyrus, the septal nuclei, and the habenula.[54,pp.536-537] A review of the primary structures of the limbic system and their interactive relationships follows.

The Thalamo-Amygdala-Hippocampal Pathway

The **thalamus** is that part of the cerebrum that sits on the top of the midbrain and serves as *the central relay station* for sensory input received from the lower part of the body and from the sensory organs. The thalamus passes on these raw stimuli to specialized brain structures, such as the amygdala and the neocortex.[55,p.226]

Sensory input sent from the thalamus travels to the amygdala significantly faster than to the frontal lobe of the neocortex.[56,pp.275-276; 57,p.122] Van der Kolk suggests possibly even seven times faster.[58; 59, p.165] In addition, the neocortex takes time to recognize and make sense of the stimuli, whereas the amygdala sounds an immediate alarm that may spark a "fight, flight, or freeze" response. In a dangerous situation, the amygdala's almost-instantaneous response could mean the difference between life and death. The significance of this difference can be recognized by a simple event:

> *Imagine walking in the woods. A crackling sound occurs. It goes straight to the amygdala through the thalamic pathway. The sound also goes from the thalamus to the cortex, which recognizes the sound to be a dry twig that snapped under the weight of your boot, or that of a rattlesnake shaking its tail. But by the time the cortex has figured this out, the amygdala is already starting to defend against the snake.*[59,pp.163-165]

The **amygdala** is a little almond-shaped structure in the limbic system located deep within the brain that serves two primary tasks. First, like *an emergency warning system,* it performs an important surveillance function by monitoring sensory stimuli throughout the brain, searching for any input that represents a threat or the need for action. So, for example, when a sleeping person hears a suspicious noise at night, the amygdala notices the unfamiliar sound and alerts the body's arousal system which quickens the person's pulse and triggers a surge of fear that makes the person's eyes snap open.[53,p.45; 57,p.61]

The amygdala is especially attuned to look for danger. As such, it is the fundamental mechanism of fear, and orchestrates the initial behavioral, physiological, and psychological responses to it.[60,pp.293-294] Joseph LeDoux, Professor of Science at the Center for Neural Science at New York University, explains how this system functions. "The amygdala is like the hub of a wheel. It receives low-level inputs from sensory-specific regions of the thalamus, higher level information from the sensory-specific cortex, and still higher level (sensory independent) information about the general situation from the hippocampus. Through such connections, the amygdala is able to process the emotional significance of individual stimuli as well as complex situations."[59,pp.168-169] In this way, the amygdala gives emotional significance to sensory input from the body (i.e., is a stimulus a threat?), then relays those evaluations to the hippocampus (which organizes the information and links it with memories of similar sensory input) and to the neocortex (which analyzes the input and gives it personal meaning). The amygdala also sends input to the hypothalamus that activates hypothalamic functions if a threat is perceived and action should be taken.[53,p.45] LeDoux further proposes:

> *Since input from the thalamus arrives at the amygdala before information from the neocortex, this earlier-arriving sensory input from the thalamus "prepares" the amygdala*

> *to process the later-arriving information from the cortex. Thus, the emotional evaluation of sensory input precedes conscious emotional experience: People may become autonomically and hormonally activated before they are able to make a conscious appraisal of what they are reacting to.*[60,p.294]

A second function of the amygdala is that it works like *an emotional computer* that links memory images with emotional states. The more significance that incoming sensory stimuli have, the more closely the input will be attended to by the amygdala, and the more strongly a memory will be retained.[60,p.295] More simply stated, "emotions amplify memories."[57,p.222] Emotionally laden memories are like snapshots or "flashbulb memories" which are stored by the amygdala. These are "explicit memories established during emotional situations [which] are often especially vivid and enduring."[57,p.221] This establishes Pavlovian conditioned associations to both positively and/or negatively valenced stimuli.[61] However, due to its vigilant surveillance or "early warning" function, the amygdala is more attuned and responsive to events perceived as potentially threatening to the person.[62] In addition, highly emotional memories are remembered more than ones with emotionally neutral details; they are not necessarily remembered accurately.[63,p.211]

The **hippocampus** sits adjacent to the amygdala and works in a complementary relationship with it by linking emotions to images, memory, and learning. The hippocampus does not generate emotion, but rather serves as *an emotional regulator.* It takes sensory-emotional input from the amygdala and attempts to put a basic cognitive understanding to it. Also in conjunction with the thalamus, the hippocampus regulates "the quiescent and arousal reactions generated by the autonomic nervous system in order to avoid extreme arousal states and maintain emotional equilibrium."[53,p.46]

A second function of the hippocampus is basic organization and categorization of experience in terms of time and space. The hippocampus establishes how stimuli and memories are related to each other in spatial-relational, contextual, or representational configurations. [59,pp.199-200]

The third function of the hippocampus is that of *short-term memory.* The hippocampus retains information for a few minutes as "working memory," then either transfers that information into more permanent memory in the temporal lobe, or the information is immediately forgotten.[59,pp.270-277] Proper functioning of short-term memory allows the person to link present input with past experience and consequently to learn from experience.[52,p.231] Thus, in a way the hippocampus has a "sophisticated computational power" because of its link to the temporal memory systems.[59,p.200] In addition, the hippocampus (along with the anterior thalamus and septal region) is involved in converting short-term memory into long-term memory and then to storing it in temporal lobe areas.

Under normal conditions, the thalamus sends input to the amygdala, which determines if there is a threat and a need for immediate response. When all is well, the amygdala passes on that input to the hippocampus which links the stimuli to previous experience and determines whether it will be remembered or forgotten.

In traumatic or prolonged high-stress conditions, the thalamus is flooded with input which it then sends on to the amygdala. Psychophysiologically, the amygdala interprets this flood of stimuli from the thalamus as a threat and attaches a sense of fear to it. The amygdala then sends a steady stream of input to the hippocampus which retains much of the experience as memory, but is unable to organize it in its usual way.[64,p.91] As a consequence, the hippocampus gets overloaded and stores the memories as isolated images and sensations, rather than understandable experience. These stored memories become temporarily forgotten until they later appear as "flashbacks" and are re-experienced as if they were happening again.

"Kindling" is also thought to occur in the hippocampus. Kindling is a process in which the hippocampus becomes more and more sensitive to the recollection of stressful experience which leads to a continuous state of hyperalertness. At first, little events that would normally be experienced as minor stressful situations suddenly produce anxiety and hypervigilance. A lowering of excitatory stimulus thresholds develops and a sense of threat, vulnerability, and fear becomes so embedded in the memory that the hippocampus begins to replay these feelings without external cues.[65] "Neurons may fire on their own (without being triggered by external trauma cues) and produce spontaneous intrusive recollections, traumatic nightmares, PTSD flashbacks, and arousal symptoms such as hyperarousal, irritability, startle, and hypervigilance."[51,p.437]

The Hypothalamic-Pituitary-Adrenal axis

The hypothalamus-pituitary-adrenocortical system (HPA axis) is a primary regulating system of the body, mediating both basic homeostatic and emergency reactions of the organism.

The **hypothalamus** is about the size of a thimble and is found at the base of the forebrain near the thalamus. The hypothalamus functions as *the master control* for the autonomic nervous system and directs many basic bodily functions, such as the sleep-wake cycle, appetite, thirst, and temperature regulation. It also modulates physiological reactions to emotional states.[53,pp.43-44; 66,pp.559-569; 67,p.156] The inner section of the hypothalamus has been found to generate calming emotions, while the outer edge "can help create basic emotions such as rage and terror as well as positive states ranging from moderate pleasure to bliss."[53,p.44]

The hypothalamus also serves as the master control of the neurohormonal system and consequently the autonomic nervous system. The hypothalamus responds to neurochemical stimuli from the thalamus or the amygdala by releasing corticotropin-releasing factor (CRF) to the pituitary. The pituitary secretes a number of hormones, such as thyroid-stimulating hormone (TSH) and adrenocorticotropic hormone (ACTH). ACTH, in turn, induces the adrenals to release steroid hormones called glucocorticoids into the bloodstream. These glucocorticoids, especially cortisol, produce a counter-stress reaction and stimulate active coping behaviors in the organism.[68] Whenever a build-up of cortisol occurs in the blood, this condition triggers neurons in the hypothalamus that inhibit the cascade of CRF and ACTH which then reduce cortisol production. Thus a negative feedback loop exists by which the system adjusts and regulates itself in order to maintain homeostasis and equilibrium of the HPA processes.[69,p.278] In addition, other hormonal pathways (including the noradrenergic, serotonergic, dopaminergic, and cholinergic) also have terminations in the hypothalamus, thereby creating a series of additional feedback loops.[55,p.488]

With traumatic stress (whether real or replayed), the thalamus floods the hypothalamus with input which one might expect would raise cortisol levels even higher. But in fact, just the opposite has been found to be true. Instead, stimuli sent to the hypothalamus overload the HPA system and the self-regulatory feedback loop loses efficiency. An "enhanced" or more sensitive negative feedback loop develops. While *acute* stress activates the HPA axis and increases glucocorticoid levels, *chronic* stress results in "(1) lower cortisol levels, (2) increased glucocorticoid receptor sensitivity, (3) stronger negative feedback inhibition, and (4) the hypothalamic-pituitary axis (HPA) system becomes progressively more sensitized."[70,p.250] In addition, there is a decreased glucocorticoid secretion in response to subsequent stress. Neuropsychiatrist Matthew Friedman, of the National Center for PTSD, notes that this HPA axis dysregulation "is a distinctive abnormality of PTSD that sets it apart from other psychiatric disorders."[71,p.46]

Dysregulation of stress hormones such as cortisol, vasopressin and oxytocin, as well as the endogenous opioids and catecholamines may induce desensitization in the adrenals and pituitary. As a consequence, "people with PTSD, like chronically and inescapably shocked animals, seem to suffer from a persistent activation of the biological stress response upon exposure to stimuli reminiscent of the trauma."[49,p.S52] This condition leaves people feeling deeply exhausted while still in a highly aroused, hypervigilant state.

Dysregulation of the HPA system leads to symptoms such as hyperarousal, anxiety, insomnia, hyperreactivity, excessive startle responses, and panic attacks. Additional symptoms include intrusive memories accompanied by dissociated or avoidant/numbing symptoms.

2. NEUROCHEMICAL SYSTEMS

Interactive networks of hormonal and neurotransmitter systems play a primary role in the normal homeostasis of the organism. These systems have multiple feedback loops which seek to maintain an equilibrium among the body's various organs, glands, muscles, tissues, and neural processes. Writing in *Harrison's Principles of Internal Medicine,* Larry Jameson of the Northwestern University Medical School describes this relationship: "The immune and endocrine systems are also intimately intertwined. The adrenal glucocorticoid, cortisol, is a powerful immunosuppressant. Cytokines and interleukins have profound effects on the functions of the pituitary, adrenal, thyroid, and gonads."[72,p.2019]

Extreme or chronic stress as experienced with PTSD can lead to significant changes and consequent dysregulation of these chemical balances and interrelationships. The following summarizes the neurochemical conditions and changes found in people experiencing PTSD. To understand these relationships, however, requires a brief preliminary note on the source and function of neurohormones and neurotransmitters.

Neurohormones are substances which travel through the bloodstream in order to affect the target endocrine glands they control, such as the adrenals, thyroid, gonads, and the part of the pancreas that produces insulin. Their primary task is to control the rates of reactions or secretions in the glands. Some hormonal effects occur in seconds, while others require several days simply to start and then continue for weeks, months, or even years.

Neurotransmitters differ from neurohormones in that they are chemicals that are located at specific neural synapses and enable the associated neurons to communicate with one another. Besides facilitating synaptic messages, neurotransmitters also stimulate glands and hormones, which in turn affect immune processes.

Repeated stimulation of specific neurons and the development of more connections by neurotransmitters causes the flow of neural information across synapses to be strengthened and learning to take place.[64,p.90] Neurochemically, learning is the creation of neural chains that enable certain feelings, thoughts or movements to be more easily evoked or replayed.[73,p.81]

A number of biochemicals serve a dual function, operating as both hormones and as neurotransmitters. Norepinephrine, for example, acts as a hormone which is secreted during vigorous exercise or anger. In this way, it acts as a stress hormone released by cells in the middle or medulla of the adrenals. It also functions as a neurotransmitter when it is secreted by both brain cells and sympathetic nerve fibers.[74,pp.87-88] Therefore, dual-function chemicals may be referred to as either hormones or neurotransmitters, depending upon the context.

Stress can be defined as the physical or mental tension that arises from perceived or actual challenges to a person's well-being or comfort. Clinically understood, stress is "a negative emotional experience accompanied by predictable biochemical, physiological, and behavioral changes that are directed toward adaptation either by manipulating the situation to alter the stressor or by accommodating its effects."[75]

Under normal stress, the body responds by releasing a number of endogenous, stress-responsive neurohormones. Epinephrine and norepinephrine [NE], serotonin, cortisol and other glucocorticoids, vasopressin, oxytocin, and endogenous opioids are released to help the organism mobilize the energy required to deal with the stress. The "fight-or-flight" emergency system is thereby activated. It "prepares for action by increases in skeletal muscle tone and sympathetic nervous system activity. The rate and the strength of the heartbeat increase, allowing oxygen to be pumped more rapidly into the cells of the muscles. The liver releases stored sugar for the use of the muscles. The blood supply shifts from the skin and viscera to irrigate the muscles and brain. Respiration quickens. The blood's ability to seal wounds is increased. We are ready to move in any direction, to hit with maximum strength, or to run as quickly as possible."[76,pp.64-65]

In most cases, when the stressor diminishes or disappears, the emergency response system shuts down and the neurochemical systems return to normal. And if the stressor does not abate, the body seeks a best-case homeostatic adjustment to the stress condition.

Under severe or chronic stress, however, these neurochemical processes become dysregulated and on-going. The body may not be able to adjust sufficiently and maintain a counteractive response over an extended period of time. That's when the symptoms of PTSD may arise and become embedded. However, Rachel Yehuda of the Mount Sinai School of Medicine in New York makes an important clinical observation. PTSD is not a universal response to stress. "Less than half of those exposed to traumatic events develop this disorder, and less than half of those fail to show remission with a few years. Therefore, it is probably appropriate to think about PTSD, particularly chronic PTSD, as a particular type of, rather than an inevitable response to, traumatic exposure."[77,p.361]

The following is a brief review of the neurochemicals which are central to the body's emergency response systems and, when dysregulated, can be clinical indicators of PTSD.

Corticotropin-Releasing Factor

As mentioned previously, corticotropin-releasing factor (CRF) is a neuropeptide produced by the hypothalamus which acts as the ignition switch for the human stress response. As such, it stimulates a number of central psychoneural systems such as the thalamo-amygdala-hippocampal pathway, the HPA axis, and "a complex cascade of reactions mediated by many other neurotransmitter, neurohormonal, immunological and metabolic mechanisms including: adrenergic, serotoneric, opioid, glutamatergic, gabergic, cholinergic, and cytokine systems."[51,p.428]

Friedman suggests that dysregulation of CRF may be the most significant abnormality in PTSD because CRF dysregulation leads to a chain reaction of dysregulation in all of these other psychoneurological systems.[78,p.33] This is, in fact, what occurs with persons experiencing PTSD. They have been found to have higher than usual levels of CRF which leads to a hypersensitivity of the HPA system and hyperstimulation of these numerous other systems.[70,p.250]

Norepinephrine

Norepinephrine (NE) is a neurohormone that is secreted by the adrenals, the locus coeruleus, and certain neurons and distributed through much of the central nervous system, particularly the organs of the limbic system, where it enhances alertness and plays a role in the consolidation of memory, especially during emotional events.[57,p.313]

Norepinephrine's primary role is to act as a global arousal hormone and initiate fight-or-flight behaviors.[79,p.108] Norepinephrine is like an accelerator pedal on a car that carries the "go" message to the sympathetic nervous system to respond to an emergency.

Norepinephrine is also a neurotransmitter in that it acts as a general facilitator in the brain to enhance problem-solving. "Norepinephrine alerts the whole brain to the crisis at hand, and the cortex is mobilized to think out how best to respond to ensure survival."[80,p.51]

It has been found that "both very low and very high levels of NE [norepinephrine] activity interfere with memory storage. The excessive fluctuations of NE levels in the stress response are likely to play a corresponding role in creating both the hypernesias and amnesias characteristic of PTSD."[81,p.234] In a review of the literature on the psychobiology of PTSD, Laurence Katz et al. highlight and explain this dysregulation of NE levels:

> *With an acute stress response, there is a massive uptake of NE from the synaptic space, resulting in a rapidly established and relatively permanent augmentation of monosynaptic evoked responses. This massive uptake of NE is hypothesized to overwhelm the NE production capabilities, causing a net depletion of synaptic NE. This depletion results in a secondary proliferation of NE receptors that are supersensitized. In turn, a relatively permanent pathway may be created among the locus coeruleus, the amygdala, and the associative memory storage areas of the brain. This neuroanatomical alteration appears to be remarkably resistant to neural*

> *mechanisms involved in response reduction or extinction.*[81,p.234]

In other words, dysregulation of norepinephrine leads to memory dysfunction and intrusive experiences. NE dysregulation also sparks emergency reactions that tend to continue on their own, far after the immediate crisis has passed. This accounts for the kindling effect that is set in motion with the hippocampus. "The continuous presence of norepinephrine appears to change the nerves in the limbic system in such a way that little events that would normally be shrugged off as minor stressful situations suddenly produce a full-blown case of 'frayed nerves,'" explains Raymond Flannery of the Department of Psychiatry at Harvard Medical School. "Both the negative and positive events of life may produce the small increments of norepinephrine that bring about the unpleasant arousal and vigilance. . . . The victim essentially develops a case of chronic overarousal, and can never 'relax.'"[80,pp.53-54]

Epinephrine

Epinephrine (also known as adrenalin) is similar to norepinephrine in that it is a biochemical messenger produced by the adrenals that acts as both a hormone and neurotransmitter. Secreted by the adrenal gland, epinephrine works as a hormone to quickly mobilize the body to respond to any stressful event. It stimulates the heart rate, muscle tone, and breathing while it increases the metabolism of glucose for needed energy.[80,pp.48-49]

Epinephrine increases when a person is anxious or faces unpredictable situations or senses a loss of control. Persons with PTSD have been found to have elevated epinephrine which in excessive amounts can interfere with the cells in our immune system as well.[74,p.88]

Serotonin

Serotonin (5-hydroxytryptophan or 5-HT) is an excitatory neurotransmitter produced by neurons in the brain which innervate the avoidance responses of the amygdala, the resilience and stress-adaptation responses in the hippocampus, and the activation responses in the hypothalamus and the adrenals.[82,pp.411-412] Van der Kolk points out that in normal functioning "serotonin plays a role in the capacity to monitor the environment flexibly and to respond with behaviors that are situation-appropriate, instead of reacting to internal stimuli that are irrelevant to current demands."[52,p.224] Furthermore, when serotonin is in adequate supply, "the person is calm, relaxed, and generally content."[80,p.48]

Under normal stress, serotonin levels may decrease and the behavioral inhibition system become lessened. In this case, a person may become unhappy, irritable, angry, or somewhat depressed.[80,p.48]

Severe traumatic stress, however, causes serotonin stores to be dysregulated or depleted. Friedman identifies the psychoneurological consequences of this abnormal serotonin function. "5-HT affects many fundamental brain mechanisms that are altered in PTSD, including sleep regulation, aggression, . . . anxiety, mood, and neuroendocrine secretion. Most notably, 5-HT neurons have direct effects on both adrenergic and HPA function."[71,p.46]

The psychological consequences of this serotonergic dysregulation are explained by van der Kolk. "Stress-induced serotonin dysfunction may lead to impaired functioning of the behavioral inhibition system; this may be related to various behavior problems seen in PTSD, including impulsivity, aggressive outbursts, compulsive reenactment of trauma-related behavior patterns, and a seeming inability to learn from past mistakes."[52,p.224] Friedman adds that persons with significant abnormalities in serotonergic levels may also experience flashbacks and panic attacks.[83,p.69]

Dopamine

Dopamine is both a hormone and an excitatory neurotransmitter that is produced by the adrenals and by dopaminergic neurons in the brain. Dopamine has important functions as a chemical mediator in parts of the central nervous system where it works as a vasoconstrictor on blood vessels, and a vasodilator on renal, mesenteric, coronary, and intracerebral vessels. Dopamine plays and important role in the anticipation and experience of pleasure.[63,pp.337-343]

No studies have specifically examined dopamine function or dysregulation in PTSD patients. However, it has been found that normal stress stimulates "the release and metabolism of dopamine (DA) in the prefrontal cortex, an area proposed to be involved in coping responses to stress."[81,p.236] Stimulation of endogenous dopamine levels has been found to increase hypervigilant states and paranoid behaviors.[82,p.412] Furthermore, decreases in serotonin such as occur in PTSD appear to result in increased dopaminergic function and its consequent hypervigilant state.[81,p.236]

Endogenous Opioids

Endorphins are the primary opioids involved in mood regulation and stress reactions. Endogenous opioids (endorphins and enkephalins) are neuroactive amine peptides which tend to perform opiate-like actions in the brain. They are synthesized within the brain, the hypothalamus, and the pituitary, and bind to receptors in the amygdala, hypothalamus, and other sites throughout the nervous system.

Endorphins perform a number of psychoneural functions. As neurotransmitters, they facilitate clear thinking and memory. As neuromodulators, they act as analgesics that modulate the perception of pain. They also function as natural tranquilizers that serve to calm the organism. When they are actively circulating (e.g., due to aerobic exercise or meditation), the person feels calm and relaxed, and often has a sense of well-being or even an emotional "high." However when there is a decrease in endorphins in the circulatory system, the individual may feel unhappy, irritable, and angry.[80,p.49]

Under normal stress, fear activates the secretion of endogenous opioids that enable the individual to not feel overwhelmed by discomfort. Opioids also help the stressed organism return to normal homeostasis once the stress has decreased or abated.

Under extreme or chronic stress, endogenous opioids become dysregulated and endorphins are released in greater amounts. Re-exposure to stimuli resembling the original stressor causes apparently unnecessary opioid release. Even previously neutral stimuli associated with the stressing event can initiate a conditioned response of opioid release.

Van der Kolk explains the consequences of the dysregulation of these neurohormones. "Endogenous opioids, which inhibit pain and reduce panic, are secreted after prolonged exposure to extreme stress."[52,p.227] Several symptoms of PTSD result from the release of excessive opioids into the system. "Endogenous opioids were responsible for a relative blunting of the emotional response to the traumatic stimulus. . . . Freezing/numbing responses may serve the function of allowing organisms not to 'consciously experience' or not to remember situations of overwhelming stress."[52,p.227] Furthermore, van der Kolk notes that excessive opioid release can "interfere with the storage of experience in explicit memory."[52,p.227] An additional finding that van der Kolk reports is that "people with PTSD developed opioid-mediated analgesia in response to a stimulus resembling the traumatic stressor, which we correlated with a secretion of endogenous opioids equivalent to 8 mg of morphine."[49,p.S53]

Glutamate and GABA

Sensory transmission within the thalamo-amygdala-hippocampal pathway involves two counteractive amino acids: the excitatory glutamate and the inhibitory gamma-aminobutyric acid (GABA).

Glutamate is the primary excitatory neurotransmitter in the brain and plays a significant role mediating sensory inputs to the brain and in enabling appraisal of input and its assignment to memory.[84,p.25] Glutamate also plays an important role in sustainng metabolic processes in the body, including the normal stress response. "Monoaminergic and opioid (e.g., adrenergic, serotonergic, and dopaminergic) responses to stress are modulated by glutamatergic neurons," explains Friedman. As a consequence, glutamate affects "crucial cortical and limbic structures involved in arousal, perception, motor function, information processing, and memory."[71,p.48]

GABA, on the other hand, is an inhibitory neurotransmitter that reduces the likelihood of synaptic function. In essence, GABA interneurons "regulate the flow of traffic through a given area," notes LeDoux.[57,p.53] David Nutt, of the School of Medicine at the University of Bristol in England, explains this relationship more precisely, noting that GABA "exerts its mediating effects by binding to the GABA-A receptor, the most common receptor in the brain, which inhibits the activation of most neurons," especially those of the hypothalamus.[84,p.25]

"Glutamate and GABA release always occurs in tandem," explains Nutt. "The glutamatergic input is always excitatory, while the GABA input is inhibitory, and the fine balance between the amino acid transmitters in the brain prevents excessive levels of excitatory transmission from leading to adverse consequences."[84,p.25]

In response to normal stress, glutamate function increases which facilitates enhanced information processing. However in response to extreme or chronic stress, information processing and memory are disrupted due to increased glutamate and decreased GABA release. As Friedman points out, "memory function may be altered in the direction of excessive recall (e.g., intrusive recollections) or problems with retrieval (e.g., amnesia)."[51,p.436] In addition, sensitization, fear conditioning, and dissociation also appear to represent disruption of the glutamatergic system.

Thyroid-Stimulating Hormone

The thyroid gland is the master regulator of the basal metabolic rate. As part of the hypothalamic-pituitary-thyroid axis, the pituitary gland releases thyroid-stimulating hormone (TSH) which stimulates the release of triiodothyronine (T3) and thyroxine (T4).

"During the normal stress response, thyroid axis function is decreased both with respect to reduced production of thyroid-stimulating hormone (TSH) and reduced conversion of T4 to the more active T3," explains Friedman.[71,p.47] This may be due to the inhibiting effect of elevated glucocorticoid levels produced by stress-induced HPA activation.

However under extreme or chronic stress as experienced in PTSD, the situation is reversed. "Basal cortisol levels are lower than normal owing to the enhanced HPA negative feedback.

Thus, thyroid function may be increased because of reduced glucocorticoid (e.g., cortisol) inhibition."[71,p.47]

Increased thyroid function can lead to increased heart rate, increased blood pressure, palpitations, tremors, or weight loss. Additional symptoms may include nervousness and emotional lability. Rachael Yehuda of the Mount Sinai School of Medicine in New York also notes that "thyroid alterations are also associated with some of the classic symptoms of PTSD, such as sleep disturbances, restlessness, anxiety, irritability, explosive anger, jumpiness or increased startle, and difficulty in concentrating."[77,p.371]

3. THE NEOCORTICAL SYSTEM

The neocortex or cerebrum is the largest part of the brain and is responsible for a wide array of body functions, including among them movement, perception, thinking, and visceral processes. One specific area of the cerebrum, the **prefrontal neocortex,** is located in the front of the brain and is "directly interconnected with every distinct functional unit of the brain."[85; p.35] As such, it is probably the best-connected part of the brain and serves as *the executive or CEO* of the person – consciously perceiving, thinking, organizing, planning, and directing cognitive, motor, sensory, and emotional functions into coordinated, adaptive behavior. It is also responsible for analyzing the external world and developing functional responses to it. This means that the prefrontal cortex takes in stimuli, compares them with prior experience, and gives it personal meaning. It then manipulates the past memories and present input to form concepts, which are then used to develop goals, priorities, and plans for action in the future.[58]

The neocortex is composed of two cerebral hemispheres, each with frontal, parietal, temporal, and occipital lobes. Specific regions of these lobes are responsible for a wide range of body and brain functions. The cerebral hemispheres are further divided by a longitudinal fissure, and connected beneath by the corpus callosum.

Each lobe and region of the neocortex has highly specialized capabilities and functions. "Each also cooperates with the rest of the brain as a whole in complex and elegant ways, giving it the ability to channel, interpret, and respond to the rush of information flooding the body's neural pathways."[53,p.17]

The left cerebral hemisphere is generally thought to be in charge of processing information in sequential fashion, organizing information, logical thinking, and problem-solving. Generation of symbols, manipulation of words, and language production is another function of the left hemisphere. The right cerebral hemisphere is thought to represent more creative, social, and emotional aspects of conscious behavior. It plays a central role in the perception and expression of emotion, and is responsible for "emotional attunement" through reading and responding to emotional expression in other people. The right hemisphere is also involved in "regulating autonomic and hormonal responses to these incoming stimuli."[52,p.233]

As is commonly believed, each of the hemispheres performs different functions, yet both contribute to similar and coordinated mental functions. For example, Elkhonon Goldberg, Clinical Professor of Neurology at New York University School of Medicine, notes that this is especially true for the brain's cognitive function. The roles of the two hemispheres in cognition are "dynamic, characterized by a gradual shift of the locus of cognitive control over a task from the right hemisphere to the left hemisphere."[85,p.46] The right hemisphere of the brain is especially equipped to deal with novel situations and solutions, while the left hemisphere is more involved with routine tasks and processes. While mental representations develop interactively in both hemispheres, during the early stages of learning a cognitive task the right hemisphere is more active, but with increased familiarity with the environment or task, the left hemisphere becomes more the locus of control.

Along with research on brain "plasticity" which has found that most neocortical systems "are remarkably susceptible to modification in response to external stimulation" and "learning by association,"[57,p.303] studies also suggest that the left and right hemispheres are functionally interwoven and interactive more than may be popularly thought.

The following table summarizes the primary functions of the two hemispheres:

Table 9 **Functions of the Neocortical Hemispheres** [68,p.22]

Properties of the Left Hemisphere	Properties of the Right Hemisphere
1. Organizes problem-solving tasks into well-ordered set of operations and processes information in sequential fashion.	1. Involved in the expression and comprehension of global nonverbal emotional communication (tone of voice, facial expression, visual/spatial communication).
2. Involved in perceiving and generation of symbolic representation by breaking down a stimulus into categorical elements and combining them into novel images.	2. Early maturation of right hemisphere consistent with importance of emotional communication in life.
3. Manipulates words and symbols that transcribe personal experience into culturally shared meaning.	3. Diffuse representational format, allowing a dynamic and holistic integration across sensory modalities.
4. Generativity is the distinguishing feature of left hemispheric cognition.	4. May be particularly integrated with the amygdala: emotional significance – fear and hostility.
	5. Has, at best, a rudimentary capacity to think or communicate analytically, employ syntax, or reason.

Van der Kolk BA. The psychobiology of posttraumatic stress disorder. *Journal of Clinical Psychiatry.* 1997; 58 (suppl 9):16-24.

Neocortical Lateralization

Van der Kolk and others have found that one of the brain's responses to the reexperience or reminder of traumatic stress is to decrease functions of the cognitively oriented left hemisphere while maintaining functions of the social and emotion-oriented right hemisphere. Van der Kolk explains: "Our recent positron emission tomography (PET) scan study of people with PTSD showed that when people with PTSD were exposed to stimuli reminiscent of their trauma, there was an increase in perfusion of the areas in the right hemisphere associated with emotional states and autonomic arousal."[86,p.193] He also suggests that the right hemisphere is thought to be able to "independently recall and act on certain memories and perceptions without active participation of the left hemisphere."[52,p.234] This means that for individuals with PTSD, emotional attunement is still functioning while cognitive processes are decreased and a sense of confusion or dissociation may follow.

Broca's Area

Another important structure of the frontal cortex that is influenced by extreme or chronic stress is **Broca's area.** Situated on the left inferior frontal lobe of the neocortex, Broca's area is responsible for putting feelings and emotions into words and translating experiences into communicable language in order to share one's personal inner experience with other people.[52,p.233]

In traumatic conditions or when re-experiencing replays or reminders of a traumatic event, the person may see, feel, or hear the sensory elements of the traumatic experience but actually be physiologically unable to put this experience into communicable language.[52,p.234] This inability to find words to explain or express such strongly uncomfortable feelings often leads to increased anxiety which makes the traumatic recall all the more difficult to handle. Van der Kolk explains the findings of his PET scan studies on this area with people exposed to stress reminiscent of their original trauma: "There is a simultaneous decrease in oxygen utilization in Broca's area – the region in the left inferior frontal cortex responsible for generating words to attach to internal experience. These findings may account for the observation that trauma may lead to 'speechless terror,' which in some individuals interferes with the ability to put feelings into words, leaving emotions to be mutely expressed by dysfunction of the body."[86,p.193]

Thus in traumatic conditions or their resurfacing in memory, the asymmetry in neocortical lateralization means that rational evaluative processes are diminished while emotional behavioral patterns remain strong. In addition, while emotional awareness seems heightened in PTSD, one's ability to put those experiences into words is severely retarded and the person is likely to experience consequent feelings of social distance and isolation.

Neural Networks

Neural networks are groups of neurons that communicate by forming microcircuits that accomplish more as a unit than individual neurons could achieve. These systems work by linking newly presented data to existing and available memory patterns. "This involves the development of the best fit between an ambiguous piece of information and the existing memories already embodied through learning."[87,p.255]

Dendritic "pruning" is a phenomenon which occurs in PTSD. Dendrites are the nerve fibers which act as receiving cells or input channels for the brain's neural pathways.[57,pp.40-43] Alexander McFarlane, Rachel Yehuda, and Richard Clark have studied the effects of stress on neural function. They define pruning as a process "in which neuronal connections die as a result of competition between neurons for connections."[87,pp.255-256] Neurons which are successful in communicating their signals or combining with other neurons to form functional networks that are reinforced by chemical repetition and pathway usage account for the pruning of other neurons. Some modification of dendritic connections can occur without significant disruption of network function. But neurons that are significantly overused or underused loose strength and viability. They can die from dysregulation.

McFarlane and associates further found that "in PTSD, the pathologic process of repeatedly replaying the trauma in one's mind likely causes, through cortical and subcortical interconnections, abnormal pruning in the related networks, consequently leading to the development of other PTSD symptoms."[87,p.256] They identify four conditions that could result.

First, they note that "when too many dendrites are lost,

networks can develop autonomous foci whereby they can become activated in the absence of environmental primes."[87,p.257] This can lead to traumatic flashbacks spontaneously occurring without warning.

Second, dissociative behaviors can arise in response to the generalization of triggers that spark intrusive traumatic memories and flashbacks due to neuronal network pruning. "What should be irrelevant reminders become relevant ones."[87,p.258]

Third, the researchers note that "loss of significant dendrites as a result of pruning can also lead to the inappropriate fusion of memory networks, resulting in a mixing of what should be independent information sets."[87,p.257] This can account for the feelings of being overwhelmed and confused that people with PTSD sometimes manifest.

Finally, "the individual may be unable to coordinate and organize relevant perceptual response caused by the loss of appropriate neural network interactions."[87,p.257] In other words, clear thinking and organized behavior may be interfered with due to these dendritic changes.

Related to this dendritic pruning is neural degeneration that occurs in the hippocampus due to overstimulation caused by

PTSD. People with PTSD have decreased hippocampal volume that might range anywhere from 5% to 26% in reported studies. "Shrinkage in the hippocampus suggests a loss of cell mass. Whether the loss results from the atrophy of dendrites or from actual cell death is not yet known." The most likely explanation for this, according to van der Kolk, is that "the shrinkage in the hippocampus is due to the effects of heightened levels of cortisol, which is known to be toxic to the hippocampus."[52,p.233]

Friedman proposes that "this reduction in volume may be caused by stress-induced HPA potentiation of glutamatergic toxicity on hippocampal neurons which produces atrophy and death of stress-vulnerable CA3 pyramidal neurons."[51,p.437] Nutt suggests stress-induced elevations of corticosterone augment the excitatory effects of glutamate which results in hippocampal structural damage. From this damage, Nutt proposes, "the normal negative feedback loop of the HPA system is changed to a positive feedback loop that increases exposure of the hippocampus to cortisol toxicity" and subsequent reduction in hippocampal volume. Nutt also suggests that short-term deficits in verbal memory may be associated with reduced hippocampal volume.[84,p.27]

4. THE IMMUNE SYSTEM

The immune system serves as the body's defense system protecting the "self" from "non-self" through complex cellular and molecular interactions. It may be divided into the innate immune system and the adaptive immune system. The innate immune system is that immunity with which one is born. It is nonspecific and is the front-line initial reaction to an invading pathogen. It includes such cells as neutrophils, basophils, monocytes/macrophages, eosinophils, mast cells, dendritic cell precursors, epithelial cells, and natural killer lymphocytes. The complement system is also part of innate immunity.

The adaptive immune system is the more evolved system that is composed of cellular and humeral arms effected by T-cells and B-cells. Adaptive immunity responds to specific antigens by proliferation of subsets of cells that retain memory of past exposure to these antigens. Several days or longer may be required for a response.

Cytokines are soluble proteins that are secreted by various cells that help regulate and direct aspects of both the innate and adaptive systems and mediate inflammatory responses. The effects of a particular cytokine may be local or it may have an effect at a distant site.

The immune system is intricately intertwined with other physiologic systems such as the neural and endocrine systems. Dysregulation of all of these systems may occur with chronic stress. In a 2004 study of the effects of maternal stress on childhood development, high stress in the family unit resulted in an increased cortisol response in the children. Rosalind Wright et al. hypothesize that "higher caregiver stress would be associated with an enhanced inflammatory response, including an increased allergen-specific proliferative response and higher levels of IgE expression," thereby increasing the potential for allergic diseases such as asthma.[88,p.1052]

Other recent studies have also demonstrated the effect of stress and emotional states on the immune system. Janice Kiecolt-Glaser et al. also studied men and women that were providing care to a spouse with a stroke or dementia. A particular proinflammatory cytokine, IL-6, that was measured over 6 years increased by four times in caregivers as compared to non-caregivers. Caregivers also reported more infectious illnesses, poorer immune responses to influenza and pneumococcal vaccines, and slower wound healing. There was also an increase in the risk for developing mild hypertension and coronary heart disease, as well as a 63% higher risk of mortality for any reason in the study group than the control group.[89]

Stress, and particularly extreme stress, has its effect on the HPA axis as well as the sympathetic nervous system as discussed previously. The resultant increase in glucocorticoid and catecholamine production has in multiple studies been shown to have a dysregulation effect on the immune system. This dysregulation may be associated with an increased risk of diabetes, cancer, osteoporosis, and cardiovascular disease.[90]

SUMMARY: THE DOCTOR'S BODY UNDER SIEGE

To summarize the neurophysiology of PTSD and to apply this information to the plight of the sued physician, the amygdala may begin to become over stimulated and interpret more and more input as threatening, while also making the doctor feel more emotionally labile. The hippocampus can become overloaded, thereby decreasing its ability to organize and handle emotional input while increasing the recall of emotionally laden memories. The cerebral hemispheres can also become affected, with the left hemisphere's function decreasing the physician's ability to think clearly and stay focused, while the right hemisphere remains emotionally active. The HPA axis will likely be overstimulated, leading to a state of hyper-alertness that makes sleep difficult and exhaustion more likely. And finally, Broca's area may shut down, leaving the doctor less able to express and explain all the internal turmoil and changes he or she is going through. These changes lead to a tendency for sued physicians to interpersonally disconnect and distance because of their emotional overload and the inability to communicate about it. All of this is neurophysiologically based and occurs on its own, out of control of the physician. This causes much consternation to the doctor and all those that he or she lives and/or works with.

The Impact of Litigation Stress on Others

Chapter 5

After the death of a patient from a pulmonary embolus, one physician wrote of his litigation experience:

> *Over the next 24 months, there were moments of heartache and periods of feeling very low over having lost a patient and good friend of many years. . . .Anger, fear of the unknown, frustration, and anxiety produced untold hours of insomnia – hours during which I agonized over questions such as: How can I best handle this burden for which I was totally unprepared? Who do I dare discuss this with? Shall I tell my family, closest friends, colleagues, professional contacts? The next 3 years proved to be a series of events that could best be described as an 'emotional rollercoaster.' Through depositions, interrogations, more depositions with a 2nd*

> *'expert witness' and interminable delays. The psychologic stress that occurred during those 3 years included anxiety, apprehension, moments of despair, loneliness, anger, fear, insomnia, mood swings, frustration, irritability, impatience – interspersed with rare moments in which I was able to overcome all those feelings and convince myself that I have been, still am, and will continue to be a competent, caring physician.*[91,p.659]

The emotional ups and downs that sued physicians go through can feel like a bone-jarring rollercoaster ride that shakes and changes direction with little forewarning. Embroiled in litigation, physicians may feel in control one day and see patients with professional ease, but after receiving a call from their attorney, become tense and preoccupied. They may find it difficult to stay focused on their medical responsibilities.

The emotional turmoil and unpredictable behaviors sued physicians experience can seriously affect their interactions with colleagues, staff, and patients, and detract from their overall medical practice.[92,pp.83-84] Legal worries and unpredictable mood swings can also make physicians hard to live with. This chapter focuses on the toll that litigation can have on a physician's family, patients, and practice.

IMPACT ON COLLEAGUES AND STAFF

An emotional ripple effect spreads to one's colleagues, staff, and patients when a litigation crisis hits. According to a study by Charles and associates, 94% of sued physicians acknowledged being significantly impacted by the litigation experience.[19] In another study reported in 1993, Polles and Neral found that of 222 physicians surveyed in Mississippi, 96 respondents (43.3%) indicated they had been involved in malpractice litigation and 22 of them were still actively involved in their cases. When asked about the effects of medical malpractice litigation on their professional life, 58% reported experiencing a consequent change in relationships with hospital staff, 63% reported experiencing a change in relationships with colleagues, and 96% reported experiencing a change in relationships with office staff due to their litigation experience.[93,p.80] Studies such as these show that the impact of a suit can be so great that people with whom the sued physician works cannot help but be affected in some way.

The nurse with whom the doctor works or other physicians in the practice may have also been named in the suit. The attorney's directive not to speak with anyone about the case especially includes anyone else that is involved in it, even if these people work side by side each day. As Charles explains, "When a number of physicians are named in one legal action, for example, the hope of the lawyers may be that one or other of the doctors will accuse one doctor of being the incompetent *one* in the handling of the case. As a result, formerly comfortable and mutually supportive relationships may be strained, suspicious, and discomforting."[94,p.128]

Even if other medical staff are not part of the case nor privy to the information, they can't help but notice their colleague's changes of mood and behavior. Thus the consequent stress in an office may make a work environment that was once friendly and focused become much more awkward and tense.

In addition to medical staff, clerical staff will need to schedule appointments for depositions and meetings with attorneys. It is unlikely that such events will remain unknown to other employees as well. Because the case may not be discussed or explained, the staff is left to their own imaginations. Some may be sympathetic due to loyalty to the doctor while others may have concerns about the competence or stability of their employer. In addition, as the physician experiences the continuing pressures of the case, the staff may need to endure mood swings and vented anger. The secondary stress may become so great that clinical or office employees may seek other employment. Staff turnover in a small office may add more responsibilities to the physician who is already an over-burdened employer.

Colleagues who were once sought for their advice, comradery, and friendship may now be avoided. The doctor may not be comfortable with this desire for isolation, and the colleagues may not understand his or her disappearance from their informal contacts. Again, the silence required by the case may keep a physician in need of support from asking for and receiving solace that is needed.

Similarly, the embarrassment and shame associated with medical litigation may not only result in a distancing by the sued physician, but doctors unfamiliar with the emotional aspects of such an event may also make themselves less available. They may feel uneasy talking about such a personal matter with a colleague, or they may not want to deal with such a "touchy" subject that could spark the other's bad mood. Colleagues may find the topic professionally threatening to their own peace of mind or may not want to be tainted by the guilt of association with someone whose reputation is in question. As one physician explained:

> *We're all aware that there are lawsuits filed that have merit, and I was taught that the malpractice system was a way for dangerous doctors to be identified, their practices restricted and the harmed patient compensated, if necessary. As a result, for years the mention of a lawsuit*

> *against a doctor was whispered about in the hallways and lounges and never mentioned directly for fear of embarrassing the doctor involved or adding fuel to an already raging fire.*[95]

IMPACT ON PATIENTS AND ONE'S PRACTICE

A lawsuit can also have a significant impact on the doctor's practice. When sued, physicians often begin to practice more defensive medicine. In 1989, Robyn Shapiro and associates surveyed 642 sued and non-sued physicians, as well as patients who had sued physicians for malpractice. They found that "47% of sued physicians and 67% of nonsued physicians reported ordering more diagnostic tests due to the malpractice claim or the threat of a malpractice claim; an average of 41% of both groups now refer more cases; and 20% of sued physicians now refuse certain types of cases. In addition, 43% of sued physicians and 60% of non-sued physicians have raised their fees specifically to cover malpractice insurance premiums or to accumulate a reserve for future malpractice-related financial burdens."[96,p.2193]

In another study by Studdert and associates 14 years later of physicians in specialties at high risk of litigation (emergency medicine, general surgery, orthopedic surgery, neurosurgery, obstetrics/gynecology, and radiology), 93% of the surveyed physicians practiced "assurance" and/or "avoidant" behaviors.[97]

Assurance behaviors, sometimes called "positive" defensive medicine, "involve supplying additional services of marginal or no medical value with the aim of reducing adverse outcomes, deterring patients from filing malpractice claims, or persuading the legal system that the standard of care was met."[97,p.2609] These include ordering more tests than medically indicated (e.g., MRI's and ultrasounds), prescribing more medications (e.g., antibiotics) than medically indicated, performing unnecessary diagnostic procedures (e.g., blood tests) and suggesting invasive procedures (e.g., biopsies) to confirm diagnoses, as well as referring patients to other specialists for consultations in unnecessary circumstances.

Avoidance behaviors, sometimes called "negative" defensive medicine, were avoidance behaviors designed to distance physicians from sources of legal risk. Avoidance behavior "encompasses both day-to-day clinical decisions affecting individual patients and more systematic alterations of scope and style of practice."[97,p.2609] This includes eliminating certain procedures or interventions prone to complications and "limiting their practices to 'bread-and-butter' operations."[97,p.2616] As a consequence, "experienced obstetricians no longer deliver babies; highly-trained neurosurgeons no longer perform lifesaving brain and trauma surgery; and orthopedic surgeons no longer perform complex procedures."[98,p.371] Studder found that "certain types of patients commonly prompt specialist physicians to behave defensively, especially those who are seen as demanding, emotional, or unpredictable" and "patients perceived as dissatisfied (including those who had filed lawsuits in the past)."[97,p.2616] Physicians are also avoiding sicker patients, patients with complex medical problems, obese persons, workers' compensation cases, and patients with prior complications (especially if they had expressed dissatisfaction with a previous physician).[97,p.2616]

In a similar study in 2003 by the Center for Studying Health System Change, Berenson and associates found similar trends, and further noted that noncompliant patients and low-income patients with inadequate or no insurance are also being avoided out of concern for an increased likelihood of a bad outcome and a malpractice claim. In addition, physicians are "referring more patients to emergency departments, safety net hospitals and academic health centers; refusing to provide on-call emergency department coverage;" and "declining to accept elective referrals from emergency departments and safety net clinics and health centers, especially for uninsured patients."[99]

These findings are consistent with other studies that point to an increased application of "defensive medicine" in an effort to ward off the potentials of malpractice suits. When the stress of litigation begins to have negative consequences on the doctors' own well-being, patients may feel a change in demeanor, an underlying anger, or a depressed lack of concern. New patients may not feel the shift that has occurred, but long-term patients will no doubt sense that something is amiss. Furthermore, the physician may begin to see each new patient as another potential lawsuit. Commenting on his own experience with malpractice litigation, Carl Glassman, a surgeon from Wilmington, Delaware describes this poignant scene:

> *The patient doesn't realize it, but he and I both sit with the sword of Damocles dangerously poised above our heads. The sword threatens the patient since he is deprived of absolute dedication on the part of a physician in fear of litigation. The physician, of course, expects the fall of the sword at any time a result does not suit the patient's fancy.*[10,p.94]

A consequence of this change in practice, risk manager Margaret Scheaffer notes, is that "for many physicians, some of the pleasure and satisfaction of practicing medicine is lost, and the quality of the doctor-patient relationship is adversely affected."[100,p.23]

Another response to the threat or reality of malpractice litigation is for physicians to limit their practice, or give it up altogether. Some doctors give up independent practice and seek employment at a hospital or other institution which offers physicians protection from malpractice claims. Other doctors decide that malpractice pressures are too much. One survey of 602 Florida physicians, for example, found that "60% considered early retirement, 33% contemplated a career change, and 28% considered moving to another state as a result of the perceived threat of malpractice liability in Florida."[101,p.1073] Especially problematic for patients and physicians is the fact that as many doctors have stopped performing procedures considered high risk, clinics and services are being closed due to a shortage of doctors willing to take such potentially litigious risks.[7] For example, in a study of 1,500 hospitals representing approximately one-third of all acute care facilities in the U.S, it was reported that as a result of malpractice litigation concerns, the number of emergency departments decreased by about 15% between 1992 and 2002.[102] This means that patients are forced to wait longer to see a specialist (such as to receive a mammogram) or to travel longer distances to receive care (such as when a car accident victim requires emergency neurosurgery).[98,p.375] Thus malpractice litigation pressures can have a significant impact on a community as well as on a physician's practice.

There is a commensurate economic cost to physicians as well. When a practice becomes more "defensive" and physicians discontinue high-risk procedures or take extra time to keep more detailed records "just in case," income flow consequently decreases. Similarly when a physician's mood is not congenial and inviting to clients, or when "the word gets out" and referrals dry up, there is an economic consequence. If the physician is so immersed in preparation for legal defense, depositions, attorney consultations, etc., patient-hours decrease as does the doctor's bottom line. There is a high economic cost to the litigation process that extends far beyond the amount named in the suit.

When life becomes a legal and emotional rollercoaster for the sued physician, it likely becomes problematic for the physician's spouse and family as well. A doctor may go from being a personal and professional beacon for people to becoming emotionally overwhelmed to the extent that just getting through the day may seem a success. It can be hard to hide this from the family, though some doctors try to do so.

IMPACT ON THE PHYSICIAN'S FAMILY

A malpractice suit often comes as a shock that leaves the doctor emotionally stunned. Charles writes that when notified of a suit, "doctors may be so angry and so depressed and the initial reaction so overwhelming that they are literally incapable of sharing the agony they feel. Their spouses may feel rejected, excluded, and powerless to help."[28,p.172]

Another common reaction by doctors to a suit is to keep it to themselves and try to act as if nothing happened. "Many physicians fail to discuss the suit with their families in a mistaken attempt to protect them from the stress," notes Michael Reineck, writing for the American Academy of Orthopaedic Surgeons.[103,p.285] To avoid unwanted pressures on a spouse, some physicians decide to keep the whole affair a secret and to bear the weight of the crisis alone. On the one hand, this may seem like a loving act, but on the other, it may leave the spouse wondering what's going on.

Most spouses or "significant others" are bound to notice a heightened tension and preoccupation of someone they live with. Family members experience the sued physician acting differently, being worried, withdrawn, and uncommunicative. The partner may feel put off and shut out by this unfamiliar behavior. What is one to think? How can one explain such mood swings when their real cause is unknown? Does it mean the relationship is on the rocks and the partner is having an affair, or does it mean that the doctor is losing perspective and getting so caught up in the practice that the family is losing its importance? Its hard to understand when one is kept in the dark. Reineck believes that "this secrecy, rather than helping, actually compounds stress when family members sense there is a problem but do not know what it is. An uninformed spouse, aware of a change in the physician's behavior, may misinterpret this change."[103,p.285]

It's hard for doctors to keep a malpractice suit secret from their families, even when they want to. Furthermore, it may not be wise to try to insulate the family from learning about it. "Physicians are often told by claims adjusters and defense attorneys that they should not speak to anyone regarding any aspect of the malpractice case," notes the Committee on Litigation of the American College of Obstetricians and Gynecologists. But the Committee also warns, "Literal adherence to this advice to 'speak to no one' can result in isolation, increased stress, and dysfunctional behavior. Such behavior may jeopardize family relationships."[92,p.83] Commenting on the significance of this issue, Charles concludes:

> *Most doctors acknowledge that the spouse carries the greater part of the emotional burden of the litigation, since the spouse has to live with the affected doctor. If the marriage is basically healthy and there is a climate of mutual support and a high degree of emotional intimacy, the challenge to the relationship is real and long term because of the nature of the litigation. There are many sleepless nights, interrupted plans, mood changes, and*

> *periods of irritability that must be absorbed. The marriage is strengthened, however, and the partners are drawn closer as they would be by any severe stress that may occur in life. For those with more vulnerable marriages, the pressure and general disruption engendered by the stress of the suit often are the last straw in an already tenuous marital situation.*[94,pp.127-128]

There have been few clinical studies of the impact of malpractice litigation stress on the families of physicians. Yet found in a number of studies on malpractice stress are statistics that validate the reality that doctors view their families as adversely affected by the legal crisis they experienced. For example, in one study Charles reported that 44.3% of sued physicians felt their families had suffered from the result of the suit; in another study, 56.5% reported being adversely affected by the experience.[94,p.128]

Numerous physicians and physician spouses have put forth their observations and personal experience relating to the impact of legal proceedings on a marriage or family. Writing about the effect that a malpractice suit has on physicians and their families, Reineck notes that a spouse's experience of litigation stress is quite similar to that of the physician.[103,p.285] A spouse's or significant other's experience of both the initial and drawn out process is not only legal or professional – it gets personal. As noted in an article for *Iowa Medicine*,[104] the partner may begin to feel:

- a deep sense of loss
- a feeling of marital isolation
- a fear of financial vulnerability
- social awkwardness
- a feeling of social isolation
- a need to provide support for the family, especially the children

The authors go on to call the spouse's experience of malpractice stress "the loneliest feeling in the world," and note that feelings such as these can create a fissure in the relationship or exacerbate problems that have already existed within the family.[104,p.18]

This sense of serious unhappiness has been voiced by a number of physician's spouses in articles for state medical society journals. For example, the wife of a surgeon being sued described the anxiety and anger that she experienced during her husband's trial:

> *Where do I begin to describe the multitude of feelings that went into three of the most traumatic days of our marriage? . . . The pressure seemed worse to me than years ago, when he prepared for examinations to become*

> *a Board certified surgeon. . . . My emotions were close to the surface every moment of those three long days, which seemed like an eternity. As I watched this drama unfold, I felt anger and fright. There was anger at the lawyers, who had brought this suit upon us. More anger surfaced as they accused my husband of neglect, when all he's ever wanted and tried to do was the very best for his patients. Frightening thoughts also filled my mind constantly. . . . Our home life was like a dream during this time. We were obsessed with the trial and could think of little else. We weren't with the children much during these days.*[105,p.725]

In another medical society journal article, another spouse wrote: *"We won. The years of worrying and waiting and being angry and scared were over. But there was no great sense of triumph, just the wastefulness, degradation, and sheer senselessness of the whole procedure."* The impact of the case continued on beyond its legal resolution, however. *"Our lives are permeated with the knowledge that if it happened once, it could happen again, if not today, then tomorrow, or next week, or next year. Statistically, in fact, the chances are he will be sued again. . . . We know it's probably only a matter of time."*[106,pp.723-724]

Litigation can have a serious impact on the children of a sued physician as well. Physicians experiencing overwhelming stress at the hospital or clinic may go home and release feelings they controlled and camouflaged during the day. They may come home angry and act impatient or intolerant with the kids. Children may get the brunt of the physician's temper, or they may get ignored and left alone while the physician-parent tries to recharge and recoup a bit. All of this can leave the children feeling uneasy and hesitant to get close to their unpredictable or unapproachable parent.

In a similar vein, E. Gardner and Richard Hall note that under continuous high stress, the physician "becomes less able and willing to participate in normal family functions and becomes increasingly critical of his or her spouse. This often leads to arguments about parenting." The authors go on to observe that "spouses, in turn, report their own feelings of frustration and anger, followed by bouts of guilt and depression. The spouse may become isolated and feel that no one can understand the problem. This frequently leads to infidelity or the abuse of alcohol or drugs."[107,p.64]

Gardner and Hall extend their observations about the children of physicians experiencing protracted stress. They note that "children in such families become acutely aware of the growing distance between their parents. They miss the abandoned family activities and the individual attention they previously received. This process may force them into attention-seeking activities which include all forms of unacceptable behavior, such as stealing, drug and alcohol abuse, and confrontations with their parents."[107,p.64] In addition, the authors note, "younger children may develop nightmares and phobias, while older children often are forced into new roles within the family structure and may respond with open hostility and a wide range of impermissible behavior."[107,pp.64-65]

Charles identifies another reaction children may have: "Younger children, especially, may misunderstand the nature of the accusations and perceive the allegations as fact. They may indeed feel their parent has deceived or shamed them, especially if the event, as often happens in small towns, is widely publicized."[94,p.128]

Outcomes such as these are every parent's greatest fear. No responsible parent wants their children to suffer, and no spouse wants to bring hardship to the family. But when accused of malpractice, a physician has difficulty staying calm, cool and collected. Anger, anxiety, and depression are almost inevitable, and the subsequent stress reactions almost impossible to avoid. Carrying such tension around, the spouse and children of the physician are bound to be adversely affected; a serious "ripple effect" is likely to occur.

In a more positive light, however, many if not most physicians and their families will likely experience significant tensions that strain the relationships during the litigation years, but will eventually find ways to cope, adjust, and pull through.

This positive potential can be recognized in the statements of a couple who went through the trauma of a 2 year malpractice litigation case. James Hutchison, an OB/GYN at the University of New Mexico Hospital in Albuquerque, was sued for allegedly mishandling a premature birth in which the child was later diagnosed with cerebral palsy. He describes the shock and anxiety the unexpected suit sparked:

> *My life changed with the arrival of the subpoena and the notification of a claim alleging medical negligent care. I was stunned! I did not remember the patient or the events stated in the claim that took place more than 5 years before. I was outraged! My care was appropriate! I was angry, frightened, ashamed, and worried. How could I tell my family, partners, patients, and friends? What if I lose in court? . . . If we lost this judicial process, we could lose everything. Most of all, I was concerned about my wife, Sue, and our family. . . . I was Chairman of the Committee on Professional Liability for ACOG [American College of Obstetricians and Gynecologists]. I knew the facts and statistics about the emotional trauma experienced by physicians during lawsuits, but now I was the recipient of that trauma. Concerns about the lawsuit were on my mind*

> *everyday and would arouse me from sleep. After 27 years of practice, how could this happen? We hoped that we would prevail, but we had to prepare for the worst. . . . The agony and fear of loss was always on our minds. It consumed our lives.*[108]

Sue Hutchison, James's wife and a mother of three grown children, tells how she and the family dealt with the ongoing pressures and stress leading to the final verdict:

> *I knew that I should not talk about the specifics of the case with anyone, but I needed to tell our grown children who lived out of state. I placed telephone calls to our 2 daughters and our college student son. They were shocked and tried to be reassuring that this "mistaken blame" would be resolved. . . . I had no safe person to listen to my fears and concerns. I did not want to burden Jim, but I knew I could defuse my anxiety if I wrote my thoughts in a journal. This "diary" became a 99-page emotional and factual account of the 2 years of litigation. Jim and I had lost control of our lives and the entire family felt the stress. . . . Two of our children came to be with us for portion of the trial, but our oldest daughter could not travel. She was 8 months pregnant with our first*

grandchild and could only anxiously wait by the phone. . . . I attempted to be a supportive listener and creative planner of distractions for both of us. We had to find ways to cope with this strain on our daily life, but concerts, movies, sporting events, exercise, and gatherings of close friends were temporary reprieves. Nothing seemed to erase the anxiety we felt. So many times during the 2 years, trial dates would be set giving hope of progress, only to be canceled and rescheduled. The most discouraging aspect was the lack of any control. We were unable to eliminate mental distraction, lack of sleep, sadness, and fear. The entire process had periods of calmness, which were shattered by events in the legal arena. Thankfully, our friends and children persisted in their support, even when Jim resisted connection. . . . On the ninth day of the trial, the jury returned a unanimous verdict for the defense. On hearing the verdict, I wept uncontrollably for an hour. It was my first release of emotion in 2 years. . . . We had a legal victory, but we were left with scars that have taken years to fade. We learned that to cope, we had to draw on the strength of our marriage, our children, our friends, our attorney, and our faith.[108]

Malpractice litigation does not have to mean disaster; it can simply mean some rough times ahead. When taken in stride and addressed wisely, it can lead to opportunities to develop greater wisdom and coping skills, as well as to strengthen relationships with patients, colleagues, staff, and family. The following presents options for proactive response at each phase of the litigation experience.

5 Phases of the Litigation Experience

Chapter 6

Obviously not all physicians are alike, nor will each go through the same personal or professional experiences when sued, but as a general pattern, physicians are likely to experience five progressive phases as they are forced to live through a malpractice suit. These include the preliminary, crisis, acute, chronic, and recovery phases. This chapter reviews the phases of psychological discomfort that physicians can expect to go through during their case.

PHASE 1. THE PRELIMINARY PHASE

The Preliminary Phase is that time between the occurrence of a sentinel medical "event" to just prior to the physician's notification of the lawsuit. During this period, either 1) the physician does not know anything is going on, but a patient is unhappy and is getting ready to file a lawsuit and serve notification, or 2) the physician knows something went wrong medically and is waiting to see how the patient responds – whether the patient takes legal action or not. Not knowing what's going to happen can be nerve wracking. The uncertainty can gnaw away at one's calm, or it can ignite a fire of anticipatory anxiety. The psychological challenge the physician faces in this phase, if he or she is even aware of any potential problem, is to be patient and remain calm. This may mean keeping focused on matters at hand while preparing for the worst.

Phase 1	**Preliminary Phase**
Duration:	From the time of the medical "event" to just before notification of the lawsuit
Challenge:	Be patient, stay calm, and plan ahead

PHASE 2. THE CRISIS PHASE

The Crisis Phase occurs during the first week or two after notice of legal action is received. Being served with a summons and complaint produces an initial shock reaction in most physicians – due to both the insult and the threat it carries. Even if the suit was anticipated, the notification can still feel like a frontal assault. However, it usually comes unexpected, catches the physician off guard, and leaves him or her struggling to keep control of unfamiliar emotions and thoughts. The sued physician is thrown into a personal and professional crisis. Flooded by strong feelings such as anger, fear, disbelief and/or panic, the physician is required to move into a legal environment in which he or she is ill prepared and inexperienced. Yet he or she still has to respond to demands of the practice – to patients, phone calls, paper work, and other responsibilities. The challenge of this phase is for the physician to regain control of his or her thoughts and feelings as quickly as possible, and to "get back on to solid ground."

Phase 2	**Crisis Phase**
Duration:	The first week or two
Challenge:	Maintain balance or regain control and an appropriate sense of perspective

PHASE 3. THE ACUTE PHASE

The Acute Phase occurs during the first few months as the physician has to deal with the suit as a fact of life, a reality that can't be shaken off. The vast majority of physicians report responding initially with anger, mixed with feelings of anxiety or depression. During these first few months the physician is likely to wonder, "What's happening in me?" and, "What can I do to get back in control of myself and regain my clarity and calm?" In addition, being able to practice medicine while being distracted by discussions with legal counsel and internal conversations with oneself becomes difficult. As the physician needs to mobilize unforseen strengths and undeveloped skills, his or her self-control and ability to handle unfamiliar feelings get tested. The challenge of this phase is to adjust and adapt to both the legal crisis and the professional and personal dilemmas it creates.

Phase 3	**Acute Phase**
Duration:	The first few months or the first month or two
Challenge:	Adjust and adapt

PHASE 4. THE CHRONIC PHASE

The Chronic Phase is that long stretch of time that extends from the first few months of the case to its end, which may take up to 5 years or even longer. This is a period in which flurries of legal scurrying may be followed by extended times of not hearing a thing from one's attorneys, only to be reignited by the scheduling or rescheduling of a deposition. All of these efforts build to a climax that may or may not occur – the case may go to trial, or it may be settled quietly (but not insignificantly) out of court.

Some physicians are able "to 'put out of their minds' and consciousness emotionally stressful ideas and effectively go about their daily tasks," Charles notes. They are able to "successfully put the issue of litigation 'aside,' especially when they are busy and occupied in their professional work."[94,p.126] However, this sense of control may only be temporary or transitory. As this phase lasts for such a long time, physicians' feelings and thoughts may shift and change unpredictably. The immediate response of anger experienced in the Acute Phase often diminishes during the Chronic Phase and may be replaced by growing anxiety or depression. These strong feelings may ebb and flow, or flare up and subside, as the doctor is reminded of "the pain that won't go away." At this time, symptoms of post-traumatic stress disorder are likely to arise and interfere with the physician's personal and professional life.

The challenge of this phase is to cope with unpredictable and changing circumstances, while having to deal with strong feelings of anxiety mixed with self-doubt or depression. To cope adequately requires that the physician find ways to plan for the times of pain and discomfort, and find ways to self-care and self-nurture rather than feel overwhelmed and incapacitated.

Phase 4	**Chronic Phase**
Duration:	From the first few months to 5 years or longer
Challenge:	"Cope" – to take care of oneself in new ways, and to persevere

PHASE 5. THE RECOVERY PHASE

The Recovery Phase extends from the conclusion of the case until full integration of the experience takes place and the physician is able to "move on" with life without a sense of being caught in its wake, either personally or professionally. This phase represents the years after the crisis is over in which the physician gains perspective from hindsight and integrates the insights gained into his or her practice of medicine. This does not mean the physician will not still have some leftover memories and emotional bruises, but these leftovers don't tend to flare up often nor stay around long. An unwanted outcome or minor medical error might occur that brings back a lot of the memories and pain, but from the new perspective the physician is able to recognize the flashback and deal with it successfully so it fades rather rapidly. The challenge of the recovery phase is to gain insight from the past and put it into action into the future so that additional suits will not be filed in the future, or if they are, they will not have the devastating effect the first suit had.

Phase 5 Recovery Phase

Duration: Closure of the case until personal and professional integration of the lessons learned takes place

Challenge: Learn from the past and continue to develop personally and professionally

Strategies for Proactive Response

Chapter 7

Knowing what to do and what not to do can make the difference between being damaged by the crisis or being able to navigate the experience successfully. As Stanford's Robert Sapolsky puts it, "Perceive yourself in a given situation to have expressive outlets, control and predictive information, for example, and you are less likely to have a stress-response."[63,p.309] The following is a review of response options that could be initiated in each phase of the litigation experience.

PREPARATION STRATEGIES FOR THE PRELIMINARY PHASE

During the time when no suit has yet been filed but a physician has a sense that a legal action may be approaching like a storm off the horizon, several preparation strategies can help the physician to be forewarned and forearmed. All of these options are based on a principle of being proactive. In a meta-analysis of 38 clinical studies of PTSD, Ariah Shalev of Hadassah University Hospital in Jerusalem found that *pre-crisis preparation* "reduces uncertainty, . . . increases one's sense of control, and teaches automatic responses that are less readily eroded under stress." Shalev concludes that such preparation training "generates positive outcome expectancy."[109,p.87]

To act as if nothing's happening, or to wait and worry, or to get anxious or depressed will only make things worse. The first and most important response a physician can chose is to be positively proactive.

1. Learn about the medical-legal process

One positive step a physician can take while not knowing if a suit will be filed or not is to start learning about the legal process. Just beginning to understand what the steps of litigation are can be helpful. A couple of articles in the medical literature which present a cursory glimpse at the steps in a legal case are "Coping with the Stress of Being Sued," by Chantal

Brazeau[110] and "Coping with a Medical Malpractice Suit" by Sara Charles.[111] There is the more extensive booklet, *Litigation Assistant: A Guide for the Defendant Physician,* by the Department of Professional Liability of the American College of Obstetricians and Gynecologists,[112] and a complete overview of the legal process in a book by Thom Lobe entitled, *Medical Malpractice: A Physician's Guide.*[113] Other resources are available through the various medical malpractice insurance carriers and state medical societies. Information gleaned from these sources can provide a clear expectation of what might lie ahead and what are appropriate legal and medical responses to a lawsuit.

It is also helpful to understand what the National Practitioner Data Bank is and the implications it has for physicians in litigation. The National Practitioner Data Bank is "a national repository of information regarding the professional competence and conduct of primarily doctors of medicine, doctors of osteopathy, and dentists" created by the Health Care Quality Improvement Act of 1986. Beginning in 1990, "each entity or individual that makes a payment on behalf of a physician in either total or partial settlement of a medical malpractice claim or in satisfaction of a judgment in a medical malpractice action must report the payment and related circumstances directly to the Data Bank within 30 days of the date of payment."[114,p.1706]

Data Bank information is not privy to public scrutiny, but as James Gray, news editor for *Medical Economics* points out, "some 11,000 entities – from hospitals to state licensing agencies to liability insurers – can access the files."[115,p.113] Gray goes on to explain the double-bind that the Data Bank puts doctors in. "The data bank's looming presence forces doctors to play a sort of roulette. If they settle a claim, they're reported to the bank. If they hold tight and go to court, they risk an adverse jury verdict. If they're dismissed from a suit before a settlement or judgment, they avoid the bank entirely. Some individual docs have stayed out of the bank by wiggling through a loophole stating that payments made on behalf of a corporation are not reportable." Gray draws the uncomfortable conclusion that "for now the NPDB is just another uneasy fact of medical life."[115,p.113]

Even though information provided to the Data Bank remains confidential and is only released to certain approved entities, national legislation has been introduced attempting to force full disclosure to the general public.[116] This currently does not seem likely but the fear of this possibility can exacerbate the anxiety of the litigation, knowing that in many circumstances, the choice to settle a case is more of an economic decision than an admission of negligence. It does, however, have implications to the sued physician as there is the potential that one's official record as a physician may be stained by the report of an incident. Thus it is important to know about the professional implications of a legal suit with a negotiated settlement or a negative judgment.

2. Study literature on medical errors

Another action a physician can take while wondering whether a suit will be filed is to study the data about medical mistakes and take a realistic yet understanding eye to unwanted medical outcomes. In 1999, the Institute of Medicine published a report entitled *To Err Is Human: Building a Safer Health System.*[117] Findings estimating the number of deaths in a year from medical errors to be at least 44,000 patients shocked the American public. This number made it the eighth leading cause of death ahead of motor vehicle accidents, breast cancer, and AIDS.

Although the number of medical errors is much higher than those in healthcare realized, the fact that a significant number occur is not new information. Much data from various studies document this reality. Richard Goldberg et al. stated that "postmortem studies comparing diagnoses listed in patients' charts with those found at necropsy have reported diagnostic error rates of 40% to 60%. This rate appears to be stable across hospitals, countries, and even areas of practice. In these studies, errors having a significant impact on patient outcome hover around 10%, and the rate has been little affected by improvements in diagnostic technology."[118] The Institute of Health went on to acknowledge, however, that it is more often the institutional networks and systems of the medical world that are responsible for medical errors. As David Mirvis, Director of the Center for Health Services Research at the University of Tennessee in Memphis, points out:

> *Most medical errors are induced by system problems rather than mistakes by individual practitioners. The Institute of Medicine report emphasizes the lessons learned from studies of errors in other systems "including the Challenger and the Three-Mile Island disasters" that system problems rather than mistakes of individual people are mainly responsible for medical errors. The delivery of healthcare is the product of a complex system;*

> *when systems fail it is commonly because of the combination of "multiple faults that occur together in unanticipated interaction, creating a chain of events in which faults grow and evolve." This is described as the "Swiss cheese" model when the holes in error defense systems line up, errors occur. . . .Although human error is the largest contributor to medical errors and there are some individuals who have criminal intent, most human errors are induced by system failures that "set up" people to fail.*[119]

How, then, do highly trained, conscientious physicians with personality traits of compulsiveness and perfectionism that enable them to perform well in the medical arena react emotionally to error? One physician, Albert Wu of Johns Hopkins University School of Medicine, pointed out, "Although patients are the first and obvious victims of medical mistakes, doctors are wounded by the same error: they are the second victims." Wu goes on to explain his understanding of this secondary trauma:

> *You feel singled out and exposed – seized by the instinct to see if anyone has noticed. You agonize about what to*

> *do, whether to tell anyone, what to say. Later, the event replays itself over and over in your mind. You question your competence but fear being discovered. You know you should confess, but dread the prospect of potential punishment and of the patient's anger. . . . Distress escalates in the face of a malpractice suit.*[120]

Even without the threat of litigation looming, the physicians' psychological response to the awareness of being responsible for an error was similar to responses of doctors who had been sued. John Christensen et al. in an article entitled "The Heart of Darkness: The Impact of Perceived Mistakes on Physicians" describe the results of interviews with physicians who discussed a previous mistake and its effect on their own psyches: "After the initial shock the physicians had a variety of emotional reactions that had lasted from several days to several months. Some of the feelings of fear, guilt, anger, embarrassment, and humiliation were unresolved at the time of the interview, even a year after the mistake. A few physicians reported symptoms of depression, including disturbances in appetite, sleep, and concentration."[121, p.426]

Thus physicians exist in a system that selects for the

personality traits of perfection and compulsiveness and a legal system that does not allow for the acceptance of unintentional human error. And when it does occur, the psychological consequences for the practitioner are great even when no threat of litigation exists. Once the threat of litigation becomes a reality, however, the consequences become even greater. Andrew Robinson and associates, for example, found in their study of 897 physicians that over 95% of the doctors surveyed reported the fear of malpractice litigation could be a barrier to their reporting of errors.[122,p.2188]

And yet there is currently an effort at hand to address this issue. Called by one medical journalist the "Say-You're-Sorry movement,"[123] programs are being developed that focus on physicians communicating with patients about medical errors.[124-126] A number of hospital systems, for example, have pursued a policy of full disclosure, such as the "Sorry Works" program developed at the Veteran's Hospital in Lexington, Kentucky.[127-129] The Denver-based COPIC Insurance Company, a physician-run medical liability insurance carrier, has initiated a similar disclosure program.[130] The Joint Commission on Accreditation of Healthcare Organizations (JCAHO) has developed a protocol for reporting "sentinel events" that are to be used by hospitals,[131] and a number of states have instituted laws allowing physicians to offer statements of condolence and sympathy which can not be used against them in court.[130] In other words, it's worthwhile to be knowledgeable and up-to-date on research and policies regarding communicating with patients about medical errors.

3. Strengthen personal and professional relationships

Another way to respond positively to the potential crisis of a lawsuit is to strengthen personal and professional relationships. The people a physician holds dear and those who are held in high regard are the ones the sued physicians will need to turn to in their time of need. These people will become the first aid stations (or the emergency room staff) waiting in the wings just in case. Therefore those people who at times get neglected because of a busy schedule need to be put higher on the priority list. The physician needs time to be with them, to do things with them, to enjoy them. They will, hopefully, appreciate the unexpected attention. Furthermore, during this phase of the unknown legal-medical concern, being with people a physician enjoys can bolster a potentially sagging self-image. Doing things with people one loves also fills emotional reservoirs and provides good memories to hold onto.

However, there is an important caveat. "When medical negligence litigation looms on the horizon, begin surrounding yourself with a strong support group, but remember the subpoena power of the plaintiff," suggests Jeffrey Hallett. "In medical negligence litigation, it is unlikely that your family, or clergy, or therapist will be subpoenaed in the case, but the plaintiff's attorneys will want to know what you have said to friends, particularly your medical colleagues, concerning the case. So the lesson to be learned is that you need to limit discussions of the case, and then prepare the ones who have been a part of such discussions for the eventual subpoenas that they are likely to receive."[13,p.404]

4. Review practice management systems

A fourth preparation strategy that physicians can pursue is to review their practice management systems and address staff and business needs before they become problems. This is similar to preparing for a long road trip by getting the gas tank filled and the brakes checked. A physician can prepare for a possible period of disquiet by reviewing his or her medical practice management to determine what could be done in advance – just in case the physician has to cut back on hours to handle legal or personal matters exacerbated by a suit. The physician does not need to tell staff or colleagues about the deeper reason for getting the business in order; in fact, that might be contraindicated. There is likely no need to talk about something that hasn't occurred yet. Additionally, any conversations not protected by law about the case could be discoverable and used by the opposing counsel against the physician at some later date. So in general, it is better to move ahead with the practice and take care of things early before there's not enough time to spend on them later.

Preparation Strategies for the Preliminary Phase

1. Learn about the medical-legal process
2. Study literature on medical errors
3. Strengthen personal and professional relationships
4. Review practice management systems

RAPID RESPONSE STRATEGIES FOR THE CRISIS PHASE

In research on response to traumatic stress, McFarlane and Yehuda concluded that "what happens in the immediate aftermath of the trauma is critical."[65,p.173] They note that during this crisis phase, people assign meanings to the traumatic events that influence their attitudes and reactions. Furthermore their initial reactions influence their later behavior. McFarlane and Yehuda also identify that "the ability to mobilize appropriate relationships and support is another critical issue at this stage of the process of adaptation."[65,p.173]

There are several Rapid Response Strategies a physician can choose when the crisis hits.

1. Contact the malpractice carrier and attorney

First and foremost is the obvious – contact the malpractice insurance carrier and possibly contact one's personal lawyer. They are the first line of defense and the ones who will be able to offer immediate information, advice and guidance for responding appropriately. In addition to legal counsel, malpractice carriers often have physician education and support programs and/or information available for doctors in crisis.

It may also be wise to consult with an independent malpractice defense attorney. The attorney for the insurance company provides the sued doctor's primary legal defense but represents both the physician's and the insurance carrier's interests. Having a personal attorney may assist the anxious, angry, or depressed physician in making important legal decisions and keeping things in perspective. As one sued physician suggests, "The very first member of that support group must be an attorney, even before your liability insurance carrier assigns you a malpractice attorney. Having a general private attorney to help you navigate the system, and to help you interpret the information being provided by your assigned malpractice attorneys, can be invaluable. Of course, this will involve legal costs that will not be covered by your liability insurance, but it is money well spent."[13,p.404]

2. Initiate increased self-care

Another Rapid Response Strategy that sued physicians

can use is to mobilize more self-care behaviors than usual.

As with medical care, self-care is a concept many physicians encourage in others but downplay for themselves. "Self-care is not a part of the physician's professional training and typically is low on a physician's list of priorities," concluded Linda Gundersen.[132,p.145] Similarly, Murray adds that "physicians deal with [other people's] personal problems all day, but they're the least likely to raise their own personal problems. They don't easily admit that they're under stress."[27,p.145]

Thus when physicians are sued, they may have difficulty admitting even to themselves how stressful the legal assault is. But it is crucial for one's psychological balance to find ways to care for oneself that are helpful. Whether this means scheduling fewer patients or taking time off altogether, when physicians are notified of a lawsuit, they are wise to pay greater attention to their own personal needs.

3. Contact a personal physician

An important way that a doctor can take care of him or herself during this Crisis Phase is to contact one's own personal physician, or to establish a professional relationship with one if such a relationship doesn't already exist.

Feelings of anger and panic can lead to a condition of hypertension and hyperreaction. These states are natural, under the conditions, but if left unchecked can become a problem later. So medical support by a physician who can maintain an objective point of view to the physician's condition is important. This brings up a dilemma, however. In a recent survey of 915 physicians, Cary Gross and associates found that 34% of the physicians surveyed did not have a personal physician as a regular source of medical care.[133,p.3211] This rate was similar to previous studies which found between 35% to 56% of physicians did not have a personal physician. Furthermore, Gross and associates found that 18% saw one of their colleagues in their medical group, and 7% of the doctors reported treating themselves. Only 43% reported having a personal physician and regular medical care. The significance of this study is that it highlights the hesitance that many doctors have to going to another doctor for help. In a clinical review article in 2000, this same observation was put forth. "The problem of recognizing and treating depressed physicians is complicated by the notorious reluctance of physicians to acknowledge their vulnerabilities or seek help," explain the authors.[43,p.72]

"Personal, professional, and societal factors contribute to

the reasons that physicians tend to be so reluctant. Physicians are used to being in a caretaking role, thus they may resist accepting that they, too, have human needs. Physicians often experience guilt or shame when receiving help from others, which may be provoked by a perception of personal weakness." Levine and Bryant offer further reasons for physician reluctance to seek help. "Professionally, physicians may fear sanctions on medical licensure or hospital privilege. Physicians may also fear discrimination in current or future practice opportunities."[43,p.72] A state physicians' health foundation echoed a similar conclusion in a Board of Medical Examiners newsletter:

> *It is completely understandable that physicians may avoid seeking help at any cost due to a number of reasons. The most obvious of these is the perceived consequences for having their illness made known to others. Many physicians believe, for example, that they may lose their license to practice medicine or have it restricted, lose hospital privileges and malpractice insurance, DEA registration, state narcotic license, have to pay increased premiums, be dropped from insurance/health plans, or [be] reported to the National Practitioners Data Bank.*

> *Couple this with the societal disapproval and lack of understanding and/or knowledge of these illnesses, particularly the "disease concepts" and it becomes increasingly difficult for these physicians to believe that they can access help without some or all of these adverse results becoming a reality.*[134,p.1]

And yet when a malpractice crisis hits and the physician is both insulted professionally and assaulted legally, medical support and supervision is one of the most important steps a doctor can make. Even though doctors are reluctant to seek professional help for their own needs, the stress of litigation and its subsequent emotional challenges should prompt physicians to seek early medical support and treatment that only the addition of pharmacologic agents can provide.

A sued physician will likely experience strong emotional responses during the initial phases of the litigation process. These feelings may continue throughout the litigation and perhaps even after there is a legal resolution. The character of these feelings may not remain constant, but rather may alternate between such emotions as anger, anxiety, and depression, accompanied by sleep disturbances and other behavioral dysfunctions.

Sleep deprivation can make an already stressful situation even more difficult and draining. If reduction of stimulants such as caffeine and adequate exercise are not effective, it may be wise to add a sedative-hypnotic agent or an antidepressant during this time after consultation with one's physician. Self-medicating is not recommended.

One of the more incapacitating symptoms that may occur throughout the litigation ordeal is anxiety. The level of anxiety may coincide with specific legal processes such as the taking of a deposition, or there may be a chronic low level of daily symptomatology. Depending on the degree and characteristics of the anxiety, one or several medications in conjunction may be needed for adequate control of symptoms. The most commonly used treatments for anxiety include the serotonin reuptake inhibitors and the benzodiazepines. The benzodiazepines, while effective, have the potential side effects of interfering with cognitive and motor function.[135,pp.472-473]

As time goes on, and particularly if the litigation is not resolved quickly, symptoms of depression may begin to play more of a role. If these symptoms begin to interfere with the daily enjoyment of life or if they present occupational difficulties, it may helpful to consider one of the many currently available antidepressants.

Selective serotonin reuptake inhibitors (SSRI's) inhibit the reuptake of the neurotransmitter serotonin or 5-hydroxytryptamine and may also be helpful in controlling associated anxiety. They are not necessarily more efficacious than any of the other classes; however, they are associated with a higher safety profile and fewer side effects than with some of the other agents. Although beneficial effects of antidepressants may not be evident for several weeks, the majority of patients do have a favorable response. In fact, neuropsychiatrist Richard Restak reports that "after one week on an antidepressant like Prozac, the PET scan changes."[136,p.141] Recent evidence also suggests that the antidepressants may promote neurogenesis and thereby reverse the atrophy that has occurred in the hippocampus.[51,p.437; 137,p.51]

Rapid Response Strategies for the Crisis Phase

1. Contact one's malpractice carrier and lawyer
2. Initiate increased self-care
3. Contact a personal physician for medical assistance to reduce physiological arousal

ADJUSTMENT STRATEGIES FOR THE ACUTE PHASE

The onset of a medical malpractice crisis demands that physicians find ways to receive care that is helpful in reducing their stress and re-establishing their effectiveness. With the significance of the consequences to one's practice and livelihood, as well as to one's personal and family life, the need for appropriate and effective response is crucial. Charles notes in her 2001 article, "Coping with a Medical Malpractice Suit," that "rapid interventions aimed at reducing the effects of stress will decrease disability, restore self-esteem, diminish risk for future claims, and enable physicians to be 'good' defendants."[111,p.55] The first few months after the physician is notified of a legal suit are crucial for the physician's long-term adjustment. A physician can employ a number of Adjustment Strategies to adapt to the new realities being faced.

1. Be proactive in the legal defense

The first option a physician can consider during the Acute Phase is to regain control of the situation and be proactive in legal matters. Doctors like to know what's going on, what their options are, and how they can positively influence outcomes. This attitude carries over into the legal process. The Committee on Medical Liability for the American Academy of Pediatrics highlights a problem physicians often face when forced into the legal arena: "The lawyer, in offering reassurances, often tells the physician not to worry. 'Just do what I tell you....' Few words stimulate greater anxiety. They tend to erode rather than support the physician's characteristic mode of functioning and result in feelings of dependence and powerlessness, which in turn generate greater anxiety."[32,p.190]

To counteract these feelings, a number of authors have made specific suggestions as to how to be proactive throughout the legal process. Mark Gorney, for example, writing in the *Physician Executive* encourages doctors to learn about the legal aspects of medical malpractice by collaborating with the attorney and taking an active participation in the case.[138] This includes reading about the litigation process and how to best handle it, and keeping in close contact with the malpractice attorney. Keeping on the attorney's radar screen by maintaining regular contact may convey to the attorney that the physician is a positive force within the case, someone the attorney can feel confident about and work with effectively.

Based on her extensive research, Charles offers additional perspectives and suggestions. First she notes that "the entire [legal] process challenges physicians' feelings of mastery as it seeks to establish who was in control of, and therefore, responsible for, the events in question. Sued physicians often experience a 'see-saw effect' – up one week and down another with alternating feelings of confidence and low self-esteem, of assurance and doubt. They may not be able to control the pace or even the outcome of their case, but engaging in activities that make them feel in better control of both their personal and professional lives and participating actively in their defense will help restore their sense of balance." To counteract these emotional fluctuations, it is suggested that physicians ask the lawyer to describe the physician's role in each step of the proceedings, and to get a sense of the anticipated length of time required to process the case. In these conversations, the physician should "make sure you feel comfortable with your appointed lawyer and request a change, if necessary." The physician may also want to "determine the usefulness of retaining a personal lawyer."[111,p.57]

Once the physician is committed to working with his or her

attorney, Charles suggests the physician take an active role with the lawyers in the defense of the case. "Prepare yourself for the unpredictability of the process – the rules, the lawyers, the judge, the experts, and the jury" and "participate in choosing your experts." The physician should also "reflect on the input of legal and insurance counsel about the case and work to acknowledge the 'truth' about the events in question. . . . It helps to recognize that litigation is about compensation, not competence, that those who are sued are often the best in their field working with sick and high-risk patients, and that most physicians are eventually vindicated."[111p.57]

2. Talk to someone who is "safe"

A second Adjustment Strategy to initiate during the first months or Acute Phase is for the sued physician to find someone he or she can talk to confidentially. As one sued physician wrote to his colleagues:

> *Hopefully, you have a family member, perhaps a spouse or sibling or parent, who can be your primary cheerleader during the proceedings. In my particular situation, I am*

> *certain that I would not have survived the process as well without the adamant and unswerving support of my wife. The clergy can be beneficial. A pastor, priest, or rabbi can offer spiritual guidance and a non-family perspective to the situation. Depending on your individual circumstances, a psychologist or psychiatrist can add much-needed professional therapy during what will be a very emotionally exhausting experience.*[13,p.404]

Confidentiality is protected between spouses, so the physician can (and most often should) talk to his or her spouse. However, it is important that the spouse keep any conversation private so as not to jeopardize the physician's case. Additionally, conversations with one's personal medical doctor seen within the circumstances of medical consultation are privileged and confidential. Further, the physician's conversations with his or her lawyer are protected, but it is not within the purview of one's malpractice attorney to provide the sued physician with psychological support and understanding. Therefore, the physician needs to think carefully about who else is safe to talk to about the litigation crisis and their reactions to it. Numerous authors in the medical literature write about the physician's need to talk to someone during this extremely stressful time, but who and how this is done deserves thinking through.

Conversations with peers can be tricky. "Some doctors are uneasy in talking about such a personal issue and do not want to either talk about or be reminded of it," explains Charles.[94,p.128] In addition, conversations about the case with one's peers are discoverable in court. As a consequence, some doctors decide that other physicians are not safe to talk with about the litigation crisis.

A physician's hesitance to talk to another physician, much less admit to being stressed out, also often extends to going for psychological help as well. And yet meeting with a psychiatrist, psychotherapist, or some other licensed counselor can be an important support system for a doctor under extreme stress. It can be a chance to sort out what's going on with someone who does not have a vested interest in the legal outcome. Psychotherapy provides not only a safe haven for the physician to discuss any and all aspects of the case, it also provides a means to effectively understand and manage malpractice litigation stress. It is an opportunity to gain insight into the dynamics of one's specific stress reactions and to get back into control of oneself and the situation.

In addition, a recent study of primary care patients starting antidepressant therapy with medication showed that "a telephone program integrating care management and structured cognitive-behavioral psychotherapy can significantly improve satisfaction and clinical outcomes."[139,p.935] As an adjunct or follow-up to traditional one-on-one interaction, telephone therapy offers the busy physician access to confidential support that may not otherwise be pursued or available.

However, one caveat is worth noting: The Committee on Professional Liability of the American College of Obstetricians and Gynecologists has warned that "if the clinical aspects of a malpractice case are discussed in counseling, care should be exercised to ensure that it is done in a formal counselor-patient relationship to ensure the confidentiality privilege."[92,p.83] As group counseling involves more than just the counselor and the sued physician, conversations may be discoverable through deposing others also in attendance. As a consequence, one study of 14 malpractice defense attorney firms suggested that defendant support groups were "too risky due to high probability of discoverability and admissibility of the counseling process."[140,p.568] To respond to this dilemma, one Connecticut physician support program chose to use a lecture format using physicians who had been sued as a way to provide information and moral support to physicians facing similar circumstances.[140] This highlights the importance of the sued physician developing a professional relationship with a licenced psychotherapist or counselor that assures non-discoverable confidentiality for all matters discussed. Some hospital systems automatically arrange for physicians who get sued to have an appointment with a mental health professional, especially with the first suit.

3. Study anger, depression, and anxiety reactions

A third Adjustment Strategy for the Acute Phase is to study psychological and physiological responses to stressful events such as occur with litigation. Often anger is one of the primary responses the sued physician has, and short-tempered outbursts are not unusual during the Acute Phase. Anger or criticism of oneself can lead to decreased self-confidence and make a physician hard to live or work with. Furthermore, when carried to the extreme, it may lead to the label of a "disruptive physician," thereby increasing an already stressful personal and professional situation. Unresolved or misplaced anger may also endanger the relationship one has with the legal defense team that is working to resolve the situation.

Experiencing depression and feeling lethargic during this time is also common. Unavoidable demands on one's time, attention and energy arise from working with malpractice attorneys on a legal defense. When tired or depressed, people tend to get grouchy or self-critical. To maintain a positive perspective and rebound from the stress of the crisis, physicians need to avoid excessive fatigue. There is also an increased need for time to unwind and take time to think about everything that's going on.

Learning about the psychological impact of anxiety and the various syndromes that can result from it will allow the physician to consider his or her own condition and the severity of symptoms being experienced. Taking this one step further, the physician who recognizes serious anxiety symptoms such as those found in post-traumatic stress disorder might next study trauma psychology. Research in this field over the past 10 years has mushroomed, and some of it may provide perspectives useful to the physician who is going through malpractice litigation.

The Acute Phase is a turbulent time when physicians need to have more time to themselves and to stay connected with those people who matter. In this way, anger, depression and anxiety have a chance to dissipate (even momentarily) and confidence can be bolstered and maintained.

Adjustment Strategies for the Acute Phase

1. Be proactive in the legal defense
2. Talk to someone who is "safe"
3. Study anger, depression, and anxiety reactions

ENDURANCE STRATEGIES FOR THE CHRONIC PHASE

The Chronic Phase goes on and on, from the early months of the malpractice crisis to the final resolution of the case. During this potentially extended time, the moods and energies of sued physicians can fluctuate a lot. Some days they are almost like new, doing what they do best - helping people to get better. But other days are hard, with reminders of the suit popping up from within or from the outside. And as these reminders rise and fall, so does the sued physician's mood. During this Chronic Phase, a number of Endurance Strategies can be implemented. They are strategies that are most appropriate for the long-haul, over the months or years when a physician has time to deal with deeper meanings and to change external behaviors or life circumstances.

1. Take time for self-reflection and self-understanding

The Endurance Strategy that can prove the most beneficial is that of self-reflection. Learning to "Know Thyself" and to be comfortable dealing with one's inner thoughts, feelings, and beliefs as they migrate and evolve is crucial to avoiding severe stress reactions.[141,p.70]

Self-observation and self-evaluation (rather than self-criticism and self-blame) are the means to getting to know and understand oneself. In addition, the study of psychological theories and explanations of personality and behavior, especially under stressful situations occurring over an extended period of time, can make it easier for the sued physician to make sense of reaction patterns and alternative responses. Furthermore, such self-exploration will afford the sued physician a chance to reflect on the meaning the suit has had in his or her life, and how it might be seen from new perspectives. Again, working with a psychotherapist can be helpful on this issue.

2. Learn "mental karate"

"Mental karate" is the ability to handle other people with ease and finesse, even under highly stressful conditions such as a deposition or a trial. Being able to read people quickly is an art most physicians develop. But being able to read the subtle cues of others across a room when feeling under the microscope of criticism is a high art most people seldom develop. This is an important skill for a sued physician responding to a deposing attorney trying to set a trap.

Similarly, starting early to master the art of not being caught off guard and not being tricked into saying something that was not intended is an important skill to have for the legal arena. To be able to speak directly when it's useful, or more subtly when it's needed, is part of the art. This is important to patient care and bedside manner. But needing to speak spontaneously in public where one's comments may be picked apart and countered can be a trying experience for anyone. So learning to think quickly when being criticized or when one's professional efforts are under the microscope of a deposition or jury's eye is a skill few physicians developed in medical school.

There are a number of articles and books that provide suggestions for responding effectively to a plaintiff's attorney or the courtroom judge. For example, in a book entitled *Medical Malpractice: A Physicians' Sourcebook,* David Horan has written about aspects of physicians' attitude, demeanor, and communication skills which make them more or less formidable as defendants.[142] Similarly, Jonathan Epstein has written about the strategies and techniques of plaintiff attorneys with suggestions for how to avoid the traps they set while at the same time, making one's own testimony more compelling.[143] Studying materials such as these can give sued physicians a framework for understanding what's going on and for staying focused and unflappable durning deposition and trial.

Being able to study psychology, and possibly working with a professional skilled in interpersonal communications under stressful conditions may provide the sued physician with a needed layer of confidence and protection to succeed at handling the stress of litigation without being scarred by it.

3. Practice "smart medicine"

Another way to avoid compounding one's professional dilemma is to practice "smart medicine." Smart medicine is the handling of one's practice in a realistic and astute manner.

When sued, some physicians tend to become overly cautious and to practice defensive medicine. The U.S. Department of Health, Education and Welfare considers defensive medicine to be "the alteration of modes of medical practice, induced by the threat of liability, for the principal purposes of forestalling the possibility of lawsuits by patients as well as providing a good legal defense in the event such lawsuits are instituted."[144] "Smart medicine," on the other hand, refers to the thoroughness one can use to help patients get better, while paying attention to details and records so that errors are less likely to happen.

Smart medicine, however, goes beyond good risk management. It can include the extra efforts a physician puts in to bolster the practice. During the Chronic Phase, for example, when a physician's time and attention can be drawn away from business and staff matters, use of a medical practice consultant might be appropriate. Such a person might focus his or her efforts on the management side of the practice in order to free the physician's time to focus on patient care. This can also serve as insurance of a kind against staff problems arising due to a sued physician's distractions or disinterest.

A symptom that physicians need to keep alert to during the Chronic Phase is the tendency to work too many hours in an effort to block out internal thoughts or external realities of litigation. This can lead to either *compassion fatigue or burnout.*

Compassion fatigue is the deep fatigue that comes from trying to help too many people who are ill. It manifests itself as physical, emotional, and spiritual exhaustion. Compassion-fatigued physicians work harder and longer and "continue to give to others until they're completely tapped out," explains John-Henry Pfefferling, director of the Center for Professional Well-Being in Durham, North Carolina. "To compensate, many physicians try to do several things at once (e.g., eat lunch while dictating chart notes and returning phone calls). And to make more time, they tend to eliminate the very things that would help revitalize them: regular exercise, interests outside of medicine, relaxed meals, time with family and friends, prayer, and meditation."[145] Physicians suffering from compassion fatigue "don't know when to stop" and get "all used up."

Burnout, on the other hand, is a state of chronic exhaustion that leads to disinterest and even dislike in what one is doing. Physicians feeling burnt out are "just going through the motions." Anderson Spickard and associates explain that "the symptoms and signs of burnout include emotional exhaustion, cynicism, and perceived clinical ineffectiveness, and a sense of depersonalization in relationships."[146,p.1447] As one risk-management expert explained, "We see doctors who are hurting, disillusioned, angry and hopeless. There's a progressive loss of idealism, energy, and purpose. The attitude comes out as, 'I don't know, I don't care, and it doesn't matter anyway.'"[147,p.212] Doctors know that they can't show these feelings to patients or staff so they present a false front, a facade of caring to cover up a disinterest in the practice.

It is easier to recover from compassion fatigue than from burnout. By taking time off and doing things that recharge and rejuvenate oneself, by re-establishing a more satisfying balance between one's personal life and one's professional life, a physician suffering from compassion fatigue will likely rebound and regain perspective and interest in people and in his or her medical practice. On the other hand, burnout is more difficult to overcome as it is experienced as not liking what one has to do and yet needing to continue it, as if slogging along without relief. To recover from burnout caused by a malpractice case, getting away for a weekend or taking time off is usually not enough. One needs to dig deeper and find answers to difficult personal and career-choice questions. This process can be facilitated in counseling as well as stress management training.

4. Meditate and get stress management training

Another way to practice smart medicine is to take an extended stress management program. One study directed by a malpractice insurance carrier in Minnesota found that "a year after a stress management program was implemented at 56 Midwestern hospitals, the frequency of malpractice claims was reduced by 72%."[148,p.50] Although a sued physician may feel too anxious to even sit still at times, by practicing the techniques demonstrated in a stress management program, he or she may find behavioral and psychological symptoms significantly decreased and the ability to weather the lengthy storm of malpractice increased. And as one senior health-care insurance company executive explained, "There's a link between stress and liability. Calmer, rested doctors are more careful, and therefore get sued less."[149,p.210] Thus, stress management techniques may also decrease a physician's likelihood of being sued in the future.

Meditation is often a primary component of stress management programs, and also a potentially powerful way physicians can manage litigation stress. One of the leading researchers in the field, Jon Kabat-Zinn of the UMass Medical Center, acknowledges that for many years, people thought that meditation was some sort of hocus-pocus mysticism.[150] He goes on to explain that this was in part due to a lack of familiarity with the technique and its theoretical foundation and practical value. Meditation is really about relaxing and paying attention to your inner mental and emotional states so that you can learn how to let go of thoughts and worries without getting so caught up and driven by them.

Currently medical schools at the University of Massachusetts, Duke, Stanford and other major medical centers offer programs which teach meditation, and some insurance companies, such as Blue Cross/Blue Shield of Massachusetts, are now paying for participation in meditation programs.[151]

There are different approaches to meditation; the one currently used most often in hospital stress reduction programs is "mindfulness meditation." Paul Millea and Richard Holloway of the Medical College of Wisconsin explain this approach: "During the meditation, a person focuses attention on sensations, including breathing, thoughts, or particular objects."[152] Ideally, what is experienced is not impeded by evaluative notions, thoughts, or distractions. Van der Kolk highlights the value of the meditative experience for people confronted with high stress. He notes that one goal in treating people with PTSD is to keep them from remaining in both physiological and psychological hyperaroused states. The purpose of the meditation exercises is to gain perspective and distance from the trauma by remaining calm. "If a person remains calm enough, he or she can revisit and process the trauma, [and] move through it."[136,p.129]

Research by Antoine Lutz and associates demonstrates that meditation is effective in altering resting baseline and long-term EEG brainwave activity.[153] It can be used to promote both deeply relaxing slow alpha and theta states, as well as highly focused, clear thinking gamma wave states.

Meditation is an effective means of achieving stress reduction, relaxation, and mood management during chronic stress. In one study of 54 cancer patients with a wide variety of diagnoses and stages of illness, the meditating patients experienced less mood disturbance and fewer symptoms of stress after participating in a meditation-based stress reduction program. Furthermore, the program was effective in decreasing mood disturbance and stress symptoms for up to 6 months, after participation in the training.[154] In one study of psoriasis patients, Kabat-Zinn and associates found that meditators' skin healed about four times faster than that of nonmediatators who were undergoing phototherapy or photochemotherapy treatments.[155] In another study by Kabat-Zinn and associates, 90 chronic pain patients experienced significant reduction in present-moment pain levels as well as reduced inhibition of activity due to pain and decreased drug utilization after a 10-week meditation training program.[156] The investigators also reported a decrease in mood disturbance and pyshcological symptomatology, including anxiety and depression, and that these improvements were maintained up to 15 months post training for all measures except the present-moment pain. Kenneth Kaplan and colleagues noted similar results with fibromyalgia patients who experienced a significant improvement of 40% to 50% following their participation in meditation training.[157]

More pertinent to the issue of physician litigation stress is a preliminary study done on subjects with anxiety disorders. John Miller and associates found "clinically and statistically significant improvements in subjective and objective symptoms of anxiety and panic following an 8-week outpatient physician-referred group stress reduction intervention based on mindfulness meditation."[158,p.192] Additionally, in a 3 year follow-up, Miller and associates noted maintenance of the gains obtained in the original study and that "mindfulness meditation can have long-term beneficial effects in the treatment of people diagnosed with anxiety disorders."[158,p.192]

All of this suggests that learning and practicing meditation during the long drawn-out years of litigation can help physicians reduce their stress and anxiety reactions while maintaining their physical health and increasing (or at least maintaining) their psychological well-being.

5. Increase positive self-care activities

A fifth Endurance Strategy for the Chronic Phase is to develop and maintain an enhanced self-care regimen. With the stress of litigation, some physicians begin to neglect their health. They may give up their exercise routine because they are working longer hours to avoid making future mistakes. And yet exercise is an important way that physicians can take care of themselves and have the energy they need for their practice.

With the unpredictable stresses of a lengthy malpractice suit, it is easy to get physically run down. Depositions, attorney consults, staff discomfort, family stress, and personal frustrations and concerns can all take their toll. An important stabilizer amidst all the turmoil can be regular exercise. Whether it is a 20 minute walk during the day or a more serious aerobic workout before or after work, exercising on a regular basis will keep serotonin levels in check, cardiovascular systems healthy, and muscle conditioning up to par. Admittedly, finding time to work out or play a game of tennis or round of golf can become more difficult when faced with legal matters and the personal tensions they bring. Even though it can feel like a practical impossibility, however, getting out and getting active can be worthwhile. It can be a chance to completely forget what's going on, or to let one's mind wander and deal with things in a more unpressured way. Leisure time physical activity will also build a reservoir of energy for those times when demands get too great and there is no time to rest. Practicing progressive relaxation, such as taught in Lamaze classes, or practicing yoga or tai chi, can also make a big difference. Anything that brings persons back to their natural state of fascination with life will help revive their spirit.

Equally as powerful can be taking time to be outdoors in nature, or to be inside immersed in a hobby such as woodworking or painting. Developing a new or renewed interest in something which is engrossing (such as music, photography, genealogy, gardening, reading, etc.) can provide a welcome distraction and a consequent calming effect.

It is also important to decrease problematic or harmful means of self-care. Alcohol abuse can become a major problem during a malpractice crisis. Doctors used to enjoying good wines with dinner may begin to use them to numb out at night. Self-medication via prescription drugs or illegal substances can also lead to major dilemmas, as all doctors know. Drug abuse is a behavior most physicians avoid like the plague, but under chronic strain, antidepressants, anxiolytics, and pain or sleep medications are tempting and even recommended.

Caffeine intake also needs to be monitored. Its wake-up effect brings on a subsequent slow-down, which then calls for another "pick me up" that eventually tires one out even more. Excessive caffeine can bring on or exacerbate depressive feelings. Reducing intake or getting off caffeine altogether can make a positive difference in one's energy and attitude.

Under stress, people often turn to food for comfort, and over-eating can occur. Regular meals and nutritious snacks can make a significant difference in the moods and behavior. Good nutrition tends to keep energy flowing at a fairly steady pace which helps to keep emotions in balance as well. Learning to cook healthy gourmet meals can make this all the more enjoyable.

Another option is to get a relaxing or deep-tissue body massage on a regular basis. Muscle tension builds and over time can take a serious toll. Taking time to let go of that tension can make sleeping easier at nights. Sleep disorders are common for physicians weathering a litigation crisis. Insomnia, fitful sleep, waking in the middle of the night, or not being able to go back to sleep can all lead to a "sleep deficit."

Recent research by William Dement, chief physician at Stanford University's Sleep Disorders Clinic, has highlighted the dynamics of sleep and the consequences of sleep deficit. Sleep disturbances are common in physicians going through a malpractice crisis. They may experience *initial* insomnia (in which the person has difficulty falling asleep), *middle* insomnia in which the person wakes up during the night and has difficulty falling back to sleep), or *terminal* insomnia (in which the person wakes up at least 2 hours too early and is unable to return to sleep). An opposite reaction of *hypersomnia* may occur instead.

Dement addresses the issue of physicians who are "chronically and severely sleep deprived," such as emergency room doctors, surgeons, anesthesiologists, and others. He notes the greatly increased risk of "fatigue-induced errors" by physicians.[159,pp.223-224] This increased risk of errors due to sleep deficit is also likely true for doctors facing malpractice litigation stress as well. When under the stress of litigation, intrusive thoughts and worries may become the norm and "a good night's sleep" may seem only a distant memory.

Dement suggests a number of interventions for people experiencing sleep problems. First he recommends keeping a sleep diary and understanding the implications of "sleep debt." Studying the number of hours of sleep one actually gets and taking seriously the need for 7 to 8 hours of sleep each night is an important first step. He then suggests getting to bed at a regular time each night and practicing stimulus control, such as avoiding brain-arousing activities like watching the news on TV, paying bills, or checking email before going to sleep. The need for good, sound sleep is especially important for physicians who are experiencing the chronic stresses of litigation. Prescribed sleep medications may be an appropriate aid for practical self-care.

The most rewarding self-care activities, however, may come from taking more time to be with one's family and friends. Giving to those who matter most, sharing with those who are on one's side no matter what, getting involved in their lives so as not to obsess about one's own can be both healing and revitalizing. Getting back in touch with the joy of children or grandchildren, or with the loving spirit in one's spouse and friends can help put things into a better perspective and make the challenges of litigation more tolerable. Furthermore, being refreshed over the weekend can make returning to the clinic easier; coming back with a renewed spirit will translate into a more welcoming and collaborative attitude toward patients and staff.

6. Pursue spiritual or religious interests

Some doctors are religious, others are not. For those who are, several studies suggest their spiritual or religious life may be an important aspect of their stress management and self-care.

Paul Mueller, David Plevak, and Teresa Rummans of the Mayo Clinic reviewed more than 2,348 studies, meta-analyses, and reviews published between 1970 to 2000 that examined the association between religious involvement and spirituality and physical health, mental health, health-related quality of life, and other health outcomes. In their reviews, "religious involvement and spirituality" was an inclusive phrase that referred to participation in an organized religion or faith behaviors, or a quest for meaning and purpose, transcendence, connectedness, and values. Using scientific criteria for their reviews, Mueller and associates found that "most studies have shown that religious involvement and spirituality are associated with better health outcomes."[160,p.1225]

Religious involvement such as attending religious services or studying religious texts has been found to be associated with less cardiovascular disease, lower blood pressure and less hypertension, fewer hospitalizations and shorter hospital stays. Compared to non-religious people, religiously active people were found to cope more effectively with illnesses such as multiple sclerosis, burns, hip fracture, cancer, asthma, HIV disease, chronic pain, end-stage renal disease, coronary artery disease, etc. Furthermore, religious involvement is associated with health-promoting behaviors such as more exercise, proper nutrition, and less use or abuse of alcohol or other drugs. Studies have also found that "religiously involved persons had fewer depressive symptoms and less depression" as well as "less anxiety and fear."[160,p.1228] Thus it is reasonable to suggest that sued physicians may benefit from religious involvement to cope with the physical and emotional symptoms of prolonged litigation stress.

Attending religious services with others can be a meaningful experience of prayer, worship, and community. Most religious organizations also have talks, classes, groups, even pot-luck dinners that can afford a chance to wrestle with spiritual concerns or to enjoy a group of like-minded people in less serious conversation. In most groups like these, it is possible to stay as superficial as one wants or needs, or to find people who are willing to go deeper and discuss the challenges of living a spiritually committed life. Similarly, going off for a few days of prayer and contemplation – whether to a religious retreat center or off on one's own – can provide the opportunity to consider the bigger picture and get in touch with spiritual sources of inspiration and comfort. Studying religious writings and turning to literature that highlights what's important and does not dwell on the negative possibilities can also be helpful. Seeking spiritual conversation and counsel with a priest, rabbi, pastor, imam, or religious elder can provide an especially valuable source of conversation, religious exploration, and personal support.

Endurance Strategies for the Chronic Phase

1. Take time for self-reflection and self-understanding
2. Learn "mental karate"
3. Practice "smart medicine"
4. Meditate and get involved in stress management training
5. Increase positive self-care activities
6. Pursue spiritual or religious interests

PREVENTATIVE STRATEGIES FOR THE RECOVERY PHASE

The Recovery Phase is that period of time following the resolution of the case in which the physician is still recovering from the after-burn of the litigation experience. This is the time of putting the whole event into perspective, of making sense of it all and moving on. That does not mean that the physician is free of memories of the chaos, insult, shame, and frustration. Rather, those memories no longer have the stronghold on him or her that they once had. For the most part, they have lost much of their power and thus, leave the physician free to practice with a new sense of relief and understanding.

The physician who survived a litigation crisis has also, hopefully, grown in wisdom from the event. And these new insights and wisdom are needed, for as one study found, "risk for an additional claim doubled . . . for physicians who had a claim in the previous year."[161,p.346] To give the physician a better chance of avoiding future lawsuits, a number of Preventative Strategies can be put in place during the Recovery Phase.

1. Participate in risk-management continuing medical education courses

The first Preventative Strategy that has proven to decrease physician vulnerability to potential future claims was participation in risk-management continuing medical education courses. A study by Paul Frisch et al. of the data of 1,903 malpractice claims against physicians found that doctors who attended one or two courses on risk management did not benefit statistically from the programs, but those who attended more than two risk-management education courses cut their incidence of claims nearly in half. The programs covered areas such as medical malpractice statutes and case law, strategies for the best defense of a malpractice suit, and "communications concerns that frequently turned bad outcomes into claims."[161,p.347] The value of such programs is statistically significant to the profession as a whole, but even more so to the physician who remains vulnerable to legal action and does not want to go through such an experience again.

2. Improve communication skills

Improving communication skills can make a significant difference in avoiding litigation in the future. Howard Beckman et al. found that interpersonal relations were mentioned in over 70% of plaintiffs' depositions in malpractice cases.[162,p.1368;163,p.283] Obviously, how doctors communicate with patients needs to be taken seriously as both a contributive factor to lawsuits and as a major risk-management option. Furthermore, in a study by Shapiro and associates, doctors as well as patients who sued for malpractice agreed, "The need for improved physician-patient communication was seen by nearly two thirds of all subjects as the most effective method for preventing malpractice claims."[96,p.2193]

"Improved communication" is a concept that is frequently mentioned in the medical literature, but what are the specific behaviors that lead to better communication? In a 1997 study of primary-care physicians, Wendy Levinson and associates reported that "no-claims" physicians 1) "educated patients more about what to expect and the flow of the visit," 2) used more "facilitation" interactions, 3) laughed and used humor more, and 4) spent more time with their patients.[164,p.553]

Levinson and her associates noted that the length of routine primary care visits contributed to predicting malpractice claims. They found that "patients who actually sue report their visits felt hurried and rushed," and that "no-claims primary care physicians spent longer in routine visits," (mean, 18.3 vs. 15.0 minutes, which means no-claims physicians spent approximately 20% more time in the clinical visit than did physicians who had been sued).[164,p.558]

No-claims physicians also oriented patients to the process of the visit more than did sued physicians. "Orienting statements help the patient develop appropriate expectations about a medical visit. They may also inform the patient about when during the interview to raise concerns and may help to prevent patients from presenting new problems in the closing moments of the interview." Orienting comments include statements such as, "First I'll examine you and then we will talk the problem over" or "I will leave time for your questions."[164,p.558]

In addition, no-claim physicians also used more "facilitative" comments, such as "Go on, tell me more about that." Facilitative comments allow the patient to talk while the physician encourages conversation with brief comments. Facilitative questions also include asking patients their opinions about their medical problems or treatment, such as "What do you think caused that to happen?" or "What do you think about taking these pills?" Levinson et al. explained that "these comments allow patients to talk and also indicate physicians' interest in their opinions, confirming studies that indicate the importance of allowing patients to talk without interruption." The investigators noted that active listening techniques can be helpful in this way. Active listening refers to when the doctor reflects back to patients the feelings, thoughts, and concerns the patients are expressing.[164,p.558]

Furthermore, no-claims physicians made more emotionally responsive statements, such as "You look worried," or "I'm concerned that this may happen again in the future." Statements showing the doctor's approval, empathy, and concern are also important. These might be expressed as "You're doing great with your diet," or "That must be tough for you."[164,p.555]

Levinson and associates found that the content of the conversation was not a significant predictor of malpractice claims, but that the process and emotional tone of the visit was an indicator of patient satisfaction. "More laughter and more use of humor by the no-claims primary care physicians indicate a warmer personal relationship and are consistent with our belief that patients want to be personally connected with their physicians," the researchers note. "A warm relationship with the physician may make the patient feel that he or she is a real person in the physician's eyes, rather than a disease." On a basis of the results of the study, Levinson et al. concluded that "how a physician says something may be as important as what is said."[164,p.558]

Building on the 1997 study of Levinson, Ambady and associates did a study in 2002 in which both sued and non-sued surgeons were audiotaped during their appointments with patients. Ten-second clips of those tapes were then filtered in such a way that the content of the conversations were garbled and only expressive features such as pitch, intonation, rhythm, and speed remained. The tapes were then rated by trained judges who found that surgeons whose voices sounded more dominant and indifferent (meaning deep, loud, and fast) had nearly 3-fold greater odds of having been sued, whereas surgeons who spoke with a tone of voice that conveyed concern and empathy for the patients had less than half the odds of having been sued. From these data the researchers concluded that "in the medical encounter, 'how' a message is conveyed may be as important 'what' is said."[165] Tone of voice and other visual cues that physicians use have a significant impact on patients' reactions to adverse outcomes and their potential to sue.[166]

In another study of 909 patients, the use of a shared decision-making approach to patient care is suggested as an additional variable in fostering patient satisfaction. Robert Bell and associates found that "physicians and their patients are gradually moving away from a paternalistic model of medicine to embrace a shared decision-making approach."[167,p.1977] A more collaborative approach to patient care "requires openness, mutual information sharing, and clinical negotiation." Unvoiced needs of patients was an indicator of patient dissatisfaction and potentially litigious attitudes. Therefore, the authors suggest that "understanding patients' expectations and responding appropriately are fundamental goals of clinical practice that can promote patient satisfaction, encourage adherence to treatment plans, and deter malpractice suits."[167,p.1977]

This collaborative attitude may extend to the patient's family members. Jack Horsley, a malpractice defense attorney, wrote an article entitled "How to Keep the Patient's Family from Thinking 'Lawsuit.'" In this article, the author notes that failure to keep the family informed has often sparked a malpractice action. "If a patient is weighing the question of whether or not to sue, the doctor's indifference to the family in their time of stress can be the deciding factor."[168,p.149] This perspective was affirmed in a study by the Louisiana Medical Mutual Insurance Company. From a random sample of 60 patient/family malpractice depositions, 25% of those selected identified physicians' devaluing of family views and their attempts to advocate on behalf of the patient as linked to their decision to sue.[169] These conclusions are also supported by a study by Marilyn May and Daniel Stengel in which they found that families who filed claims were more likely to complain that their physicians had no concern for them personally.[170]

To avoid the possibility of a family taking offense and suing a physician, Horsley suggests the doctor invite a close relative of the patient to accompany the patient to the office or pre-op consultations, tell them everything they're entitled to know, and explain to them beforehand contingencies that could later arise. Following a significant procedure, Horsley suggests the treating physician report the results to the family so as to "never leave them hanging in the midst of a crisis."[168] Because family members often assist a patient in deciding about whether or not to file a lawsuit, attending to their concerns throughout medical treatment makes logical sense for sound risk management.

Based on findings such as these, Gerald Hickson and associates in a comparative study of sued versus non-sued doctors propose that "professional societies and organizations should make interpersonal skills a focus in continuing medical education for all physicians."[171,p.1587] Taking into account the specific skills found in the studies mentioned, training such as this could make a positive impact on a physician recovering from a legal crisis and also help doctors avoid future litigation-laden circumstances.

3. Increase wise practice management

A third Preventative Strategy for the Recovery Phase pertains to sound practice management. Based on her research and clinical experience, Charles suggests one identify "areas of practice that cause anxiety or feelings of 'loss of control' and find ways to diminish them."[111,p.57] She also encourages physicians to "not participate in practice situations that demand compromises" in one's professional standards. Situations that could lead to physicians compromising their standards might arise due to time or reimbursement constraints, or due to a decline in their psychological health and professional integrity (such as when sexual boundaries are crossed, self-prescription occurs, etc.).

A proactive strategy for decreasing one's odds of being sued is to engage in activities that will increase one's competence, such as teaching, or hospital or clinical committee work.[111,p.57] Teaching gives the physician an opportunity to think about and define patient care and practice procedures, whereas committee work provides the physician a chance to hear others' points of view while participating in larger-scale decision-making. Both teaching and committee work afford physicians the chance to put to work the wisdom they've gained in their practice and litigation experience.

Activities such as these also lead to greater practice-analysis and self-reflection, which potentially strengthen a physician's insight and perspective on professional matters. This conclusion was also supported in a study by Elaine Adamson and associates of 427 surgeons. They found that surgeons with few or no claims were more likely to be Board certified, work in a group practice, be members of a professional society, and belong to a clinical faculty. These physicians, the researchers assert, "manifest exemplary modes of professional peer relations and responsible clinical behavior."[172,p.37]

4. Maintain wellness and well-being practices

A number of self-care behaviors can be useful to a sued physician in the Recovery Phase. Eric Weiner and associates identified 5 primary activities that the physicians surveyed used to maintain their wellness: relationships, religion or spirituality, self-care, work, and having a positive approach to life.[173] Spending time with family, friends, colleagues, and community activities was of high importance for these doctors, as was being involved in spiritual or religious practices and activities. Working at a medical practice that provides meaning and satisfaction was also important to physician well-being, as was approaching life and work with a positive orientation. Self-care activities covered a wide spectrum, from reading and exercise to nutrition and counseling. All of these activities are important means of recharging one's batteries and maintaining one's health and perspective during the Recovery Phase.

5. Write about the experience

Physician recovery can also be bolstered by writing about the litigation experience and all that it sparked. Once the case has been closed, concern for discoverability is likely no longer an issue and one can write about all that went on, both personally and professionally, without the threat of self-incrimination. Writing for oneself can become a means of sorting out and making sense of the ordeal.

For most physicians, during the litigation process there was too much to think about and too few opportunities to deal with all the thoughts and feelings that surfaced. There was likely never enough time to talk about all of them, and few friends or family had enough time and patience to listen to it all. Consequently, feelings, memories, and questions probably got stored away and linger unresolved. Time does not always heal, and the trauma of the past events and their present shadows need to be brought out into the light to be understood and put in their place.

Writing can help people make sense of what happened and why it happened. It can also become a creative way to think through what can be done in the future to ward against further recurrences. There is scientific basis for this suggestion. In a 1999 study, Joshua Smyth and associates instructed asthma and rheumatoid arthritis patients to write about the most stressful events in their lives for just 20 minutes a day for 3 consecutive days.[174; 175] When compared to the control group who had written about more mundane matters, the subjects who wrote about major stresses showed greater rates of improvement as measured by overall disease activity 4 months after their writing experience. Asthma patients improved their lung function and arthritis patients reduced their symptoms.

A study in 2001 by Joshua Klapow and colleagues with elderly primary care patients using a similar (though not identical) protocol, found that written self-disclosure significantly reduced symptoms and use of out-patient services and their associated costs.[176] In a third strudy, in 2002 Annette Stanton and associates had patients with early breast cancer write about their deepest thoughts and feelings about breast cancer. Three months after the writing intervention, subjects reported "significantly decreased physical symptoms" and "reduced medical visits for cancer-related morbidities."[177,p.4160] These findings are consistent with previous studies which concluded that writing could be effective in reducing symptoms and reliably improving health outcomes as measured by immune function, subjective well-being, and subsequent health center visits.[178; 179; 180]

Based on his review of Smyth's study and similar research, David Spiegel of Stanford University's School of Medicine concluded in an article on emotional expression and disease outcome that "ventilation of negative emotion, even just to an unknown reader, seems to have helped these patients acknowledge, bear and put into perspective their distress."[181,p.1329] It would seem likely that this would be true for doctors as well – and that seems to be the case.

Writing as a means of facilitating physician well-being is currently being used in a physician support program at the University of California San Francisco Medical Center. The "Doctoring to Heal" program is designed to foster well-being among physicians through self-reflection. Part of its structure is for each doctor to write for 10 to 15 minutes each meeting and to read their story to the group. Participating physicians report on the value of "sharing of clinical narratives and personal stories exploring meaning and emotion in the practice of medicine. . . [where] mistakes, insecurities and fears are tolerated."[182,pp.66,69] The program has been so useful that it is being replicated in numerous hospitals across the nation, such as Columbia University's College of Physicians and Surgeons and Pennsylvania State University's College of Medicine.

Thus a potentially powerful strategy for recovering from a lawsuit and preventing recurrence in the future is to write about the experience so as to put it in its proper perspective, and to consider sharing the narrative with other physicians in order to open dialogue about the struggles and strains, challenges, and victories of going through a malpractice litigation experience. It could evolve into a paper or book that could be shared with others struggling through malpractice crises and could possibly help save their practices or even their lives.

Preventative Strategies for the Recovery Phase

1. Participate in risk-management CME courses
2. Improve communication skills
3. Increase wise practice management
4. Maintain wellness and well-being practices
5. Write about the experience

Prepare for the Possibility

Chapter 8

Researchers in the field of trauma and stress have found that preparation for a stressful event, when such preparation is possible, "protects individuals from the effect of stress. It reduces uncertainty, increases one's sense of control, and teaches automatic responses that are less readily eroded under stress."[109,p.87]

Physicians need to be prepared for the possibility that one day they will be served with a malpractice suit. They need to know what to expect and what are their best options for response.

Over the last 40 years we have experienced malpractice escalating from a minimal problem to a major crisis – not only a crisis for the country, but also a personal crisis for scores of physicians. That's the part that this book has addressed – the personal toll that litigation has been taking on good, competent doctors and what can be done to enable sued physicians to withstand the challenges that a legal crisis brings.

Good doctors can get overwhelmed by unwarranted malpractice litigation. Their reputations and practices can suffer; their personal and family well-being can be damaged. And that should not happen. Physicians who are prepared in advance for the inevitable will be less likely to become traumatized by litigation and more likely to respond in positive and productive ways.

Most medical schools and state and local medical societies offer short presentations or 1-day workshops on malpractice litigation. Usually these programs focus on the legal aspects of a suit – what to expect and how to respond to lawyers, depositions, and court appearances. Less often do they address the stresses that a sued physician will likely experience, or how the suit can be handled with the least amount of negative consequences. Such programs offer an introduction to the legal system but not how to prepare for the possibility of being sued.

It is our deepest hope that the information in this book will provide some understanding and direction for those who are challenged with malpractice litigation. Also that it will enable them to survive the personal and professional aspects of the legal crisis and to develop ways to keep calm, confident, healthy, and productive during the process.

If you have stories or comments on how this book has helped you or others, we would like to hear from you. We can be contacted at:

Physician Health Publications
P.O. Box 356, Lafayette, CA 94549
tel: 925-283-2693

www.physicianhealthpublications.com

jjames@physicianhealthpublications.com
edavis@physicianhealthpublications.com

References

1. James JM, James MM. *Passion for Life: Psychology and the Human Spirit.* New York: Dutton; 1991.

2. Wyckoff RL. The effects of a malpractice suit upon physicians in Connecticut. *Journal of the American Medical Association.* 1961; 176:1096-1101.

3. Anderson RE. Outcomes of medical-malpractice litigation. *New England Journal of Medicine.* 1997; 336:1680-1681.

4. Crane M. Our national survey confirms: even the best doctors are targets. *Medical Economics.* August 1999:11-17.

5. Ely JW, Dawson JD, Young PR, Doebbeling BN, Goerdt CJ, Elder NC, Olick RS. Malpractice claims against family physicians: are the best doctors sued more? *Journal of Family Practice.* 1999; 48:23-30.

6. Pasko T, Smart DR. *Physician Characteristics and Distribution in the US.* 2005 edition. Chicago: American Medical Association Press, 2005.

7. Palmisano DJ. Will your physician be there? The medical liability crisis in America. American Medical Association. Available at: http://www.ama-assn.org/ama/pub/article/print/1752-7863.html. Accessed July 13, 2004.

8. Conrow WF. Quoted by: Gerber PC. Malpractice: making the best of a bad situation. *Dental Management.* June 1991:22-25.

9. Kanter LJ. An experience with the malpractice system. In: From Exam Room to the Courtroom Symposium. Syllabus of Scientific Papers, Plenary Sessions of the 1997 Annual Meeting of the American College of Allergy, Asthma and Immunology; November 7-12, 1997; San Diego, CA: 369-371.

10. Glassman CI. You can't win for losin'. *Delaware Medical Journal.* 1984; 56:93-95.

11. DeWitt DE. Malpractice lawsuits and paranoia. *American Family Physician.* 1992; 46:45-54.

12. Kaplan GW. Malpractice risks for urologists. *Urology.* 1998; 51:183-185.

13. Hallett JS. Medical-legal considerations in the practice of allergy: personal reflections on lessons learned from an immunotherapy fatality. *Allergy and Asthma Proceedings.* 2004; 25:401-406.

14. Fokes EC. You and malpractice stress: V. A death in the family. *Journal of the Medical Association of Georgia.* 1987; 76:115-116.

15. Charles SC, Kennedy E. *Defendant: A Psychiatrist on Trial for Medical Malpractice.* New York: Free Press, 1985.

16. Charles SC, Wilbert JR, Kennedy EC. Physicians' self-reports of reactions to malpractice litigation. *American Journal of Psychiatry.* 1984; 141:563-565.

17. Charles SC, Wilbert JR, Franke KJ. Sued and nonsued physicians' self-reported reactions to malpractice litigation. *American Journal of Psychiatry.* 1985; 142:437-440.

18. Charles SC. Malpractice litigation and its impact on physicians. *Current Psychiatric Therapies.* 1986; 23:173-180.

19. Charles SC, Warnecke RB, Wilbert JR, Lichtenberg R, DeJesus C. Sued and nonsued physicians: satisfactions, dissatisfactions, and sources of stress. *Psychosomatics.* 1987; 28:462-466.

20. Charles SC, Pyskoty CE, Nelson A. Physicians on trial – self-reported reactions to malpractice trials. *Western Journal of Medicine.* 1988; 148:358-360.

21. Charles SC, Warnecke RB, Nelson A, Pyskoty CE. Appraisal of the event as a factor in coping with malpractice litigation. *Behavioral Medicine.* Winter 1988:148-155.

22. Martin CA, Wilson JF, Fiebelman ND, Gurley DN, Miller TW. Physicians' psychologic reactions to malpractice litigation. *Southern Medical Journal.* 1991; 84:1300-1304.

23. Krakowski AJ. Stress and the practice of medicine II. Stressors, stresses, and strains. *Psychotherapy and Psychosomatics.* 1982; 38:11-23.

24. Gabbard GO. The role of compulsiveness in the normal physician. *Journal of the American Medical Association.* 1985; 254:2926-2929.

25. Stilwell NA, Wallick MM, Thal SE, Burleson JA. Myers-Briggs type and medical specialty choice: a new look at an old question. *Teaching and Learning in Medicine: An International Journal.* 2000; 12:14-20.

26. Wallick MM, Cambre KM. Personality types in academic medicine. *Journal of the Louisiana State Medical Society.* 1999; 151:378-382.

27. Murray TJ. Quoted in: Gundersen L. Physician burnout. *Annals of Internal Medicine.* 2001; 135:145-148.

28. Charles SC. Malpractice suits: their effect on doctors, patients, and families. *Journal of the Medical Association of Georgia.* 1987; 76:171-172.

29. American Psychiatric Association. *Diagnostic and Statistical Manual of Mental Disorders: DSM-III. 3rd edition.* Washington, DC: American Psychiatric Association, 1980.

30. Osler W. *Aequanimitas: With Other Addresses to Medical Students, Nurses and Practitioners of Medicine. 3rd edition.* New York: McGraw-Hill; 1932.

31. Davant C. Quoted in: Crane M. Clinical guidelines: a malpractice safety net? *Medical Economics.* April 12, 1999: 238-243.

32. Committee on Medical Liability, *American Academy of Pediatrics. Medical Liability for Pediatricians. 6th edition.* Elk Grove Village, IL: American Academy of Pediatrics, 2004:187-192.

33. American Psychiatric Association. *Diagnostic and Statistical Manual of Mental Disorders: DSM-IV. 4th edition. Text Revision.* Washington, DC: American Psychiatric Association; 2000.

34. Hobbs T. Quoted in: Hoepfer M. Withstanding the stress of litigation. *Pennsylvania Medicine.* March 1997:22-24.

35. Lopatin M . Malpractice: I knew she was trouble. *Medical Economics.* June 4, 2004;81:39.

36. Weber DO. Poll results: doctors' disruptive behavior disturbs physician leaders. *Physician Executive.* 2004; 30(5):6-14.

37. Weber DO. For safety's sake disruptive behavior must be tamed. *Physician Executive.* September-October 2004; 30(5):16-17.

38. Council on Ethical and Judicial Affairs of the American Medical Association. Physicians with disruptive behavior. (2-A-00) CEJA *Opinion 9.045.* American Medical Association, June 2000. Available at: http://www.ama-assn.org/ama/pub/category/5496.htm. Accessed June 25, 2003.

39. Disruptive behavior involving members of the medical staff. *UCI Medical Staff Policy,* University of California at Irvine, CA. Available at: http://www.ucihs.med.umkc.edu/residency/intmed/rotation_curr/Impaired_Phys.pdf. Accessed June 25, 2003.

40. Hankes L. Disruptive behavior. Leadership Conference: Washington Physicians Health Program, May 3, 2002. Available at: http://www.wsma.org/memresources/ldef_hankes.pdf. Accessed June 25, 2003.

41. Arkansas Hospitals Association. The disruptive physician – diagnosis and management. *Arkansas Hospitals Magazine,* Fall 2000. Available at: http://www.arkhospitals.org/publications/arkhospmag/ahm_FALL00_p7.htm. Accessed June 25, 2003.

42. Pfifferling JH. Managing the unmanageable: the disruptive physician. *Family Practice Management,* November-December 1997. Available at: http://www.aafp.org/fpm/971100fm/managing.html. Accessed June 25, 2003.

43. Levine RE, Bryant SG. The depressed physician: a different kind of impairment. *Hospital Physician.* February 2000:67-73,86.

44. Miles S. Quoted in: Landers SJ. Depression increasing, even among physicians. *AMNews* July 7, 2003. Available at: http://www.ama-assn.org/sci-pubs/amnews/pick_03/hlsc0707.htm. Accessed July 7, 2003.

45. Rickels K, Rynn M. Overview and clinical presentation of generalized anxiety disorder. *Psychiatric Clinics of North America.* 2001; 24:1-17.

46. Green BL. Defining trauma: terminology and generic stressor dimensions. *Journal of Applied Social Psychology.* 1990; 20:1632-1642.

47. van der Kolk BA, McFarlane AC. The black hole of trauma. In: van der Kolk BA, McFarlane AC, Weisaeth L, eds. *Traumatic Stress: The Effects of Overwhelming Experience on Mind, Body, and Society.* New York: Guilford Press, 1996:3-23.

48. McGaugh J. Quoted in: Restak R. *The Secret Life of the Brain.* Washington DC: Joseph Henry Press; 2001.

49. van der Kolk BA. The psychobiology and psychopharmacology of PTSD. *Human Psychopharmacology: Clinical and Experimental.* 2001; 16:S49-S64.

50. Schell TL, Marshall GN, Jaycox LH. All symptoms are not created equal: the prominent role of hyperarousal in the natural course of posttraumatic psychological distress. *Journal of Abnormal Psychology.* 2004; 113:189-197.

51. Friedman MJ. Future pharmacotherapy for post-traumatic stress disorder: prevention and treatment. *Psychiatric Clinics of North America.* 2002; 25:427-441.

52. van der Kolk BA. The body keeps score: approaches to the psychobiology of posttraumatic stress disorder. In: van der Kolk BA, McFarlane AC, Weisaeth L, eds. *Traumatic Stress: The Effects of Overwhelming Experience on Mind, Body, and Society.* New York: Guilford Press, 1996:214-241.

53. Newberg A, D'Aquili E, Rause V. *Why God Won't Go Away: Brain Science and the Biology of Belief.* New York: Ballentine Books, 2001.

54. Victor M, Ropper AH. *Adams and Victor's Principles of Neurology. 7th edition.* New York: McGraw-Hill, 2001.

55. Yudofsky SC, Hales RE. *The American Psychiatric Press Textbook of Neuropsychiatry. 3rd edition.* Washington, DC: American Psychiatric Press, 1997.

56. LeDoux JE. Emotion as memory: anatomical systems underlying indelible neural traces. In: Christianson SA, ed. *Handbook of Emotion and Memory.* Hillsdale, NJ: Erlbaum, 1992:269-288.

57. LeDoux JE. *Synaptic Self.* New York: Penguin, 2003.

58. van der Kolk BA. Trauma and the Brain. Course lecture presented at: Masters and Johnson Programs; March 15, 2003; New Orleans, LA.

59. LeDoux JE. *The Emotional Brain: The Mysterious Underpinnings of Emotional Life.* New York: Simon & Schuster, 1996.

60. van der Kolk BA. Trauma and memory. In: van der Kolk BA, McFarlane AC, Weisaeth L, eds. *Traumatic Stress: The Effects of Overwhelming Experience on Mind, Body, and Society.* New York: Guilford Press, 1996:279-302.

61. Davis M, Whalen PJ. The amygdala: vigilance and emotion. *Molecular Psychiatry.* 2001; 6(1):13-34.

62. Hamann SB, Ely TD, Hoffman JM, Kilts CD. Ecstasy and agony: activation of the human amygdala in positive and negative emotion. *Psychological Science.* 2002; 13(2):135-141.

63. Sapolsky R. *Why Zebras Don't Get Ulcers. 3rd edition.* New York: Henry Holt and Company, 2004.

64. Sapolsky R. Taming stress. *Scientific American.* Special Issue. September 2003:87-95.

65. McFarlane AC, Yehuda R. Resilience, vulnerability, and the course of posttraumatic reactions. In: van der Kolk BA, McFarlane AC, Weisaeth L, eds. *Traumatic Stress: The Effects of Overwhelming Experience on Mind, Body, and Society.* New York: Guilford Press, 1996:159-181.

66. Nolte J. *The Human Brain: An Introduction to Its Functional Anatomy. 5th edition.* St. Louis: Mosby, 2002.

67. Damasio A. *The Feeling of What Happens: Body and Emotion in the Making of Consciousness.* San Diego: Harcourt, 1999.

68. van der Kolk BA. The psychobiology of posttraumatic stress disorder. *Journal of Clinical Psychiatry.* 1997; 58 (suppl 9):16-24.

69. Krystal JH, Kosten TR, Southwick S, Mason JW, Perry BD, Giller EL. Neurobiological aspects of PTSD: review of clinical and preclinical studies. In: Horowitz MJ, ed. *Essential Papers on Posttraumatic Stress Disorder.* New York: New York University Press, 1999:274-300.

70. Scott MJ, Stradling SG. Translating the psychobiology of post-traumatic stress disorder into clinically useful analogy. British Journal of Medical Psychology. 2001; 74:249-254.

71. Friedman MJ. What might the psychobiology of posttraumatic stress disorder teach us about future approaches to pharmacotherapy? *Journal of Clinical Psychiatry.* 2000; 61(suppl 7):44-51.

72. Jameson JL. Principles of endocrinology. In: Harrison TR, Braunwald E, et al., eds. *Harrison's Principles of Internal Medicine. 15th edition.* New York: McGraw Hill, 2001:2019-2029.

73. Holloway M. The mutable brain. *Scientific American.* Special Issue. September 2003:79-85.

74. Justice B. *Who Gets Sick: Thinking and Health.* Houston: Peak Press, 1987.

75. Baum A. Stress, intrusive imagery, and chronic distress. *Health Psychology.* 1990: 9(6):653-675.

76. Ornstein RS, Sobel D. *The Healing Brain.* New York: Simon & Schuster, 1987.

77. Yehuda R. Psychoneuroendocrinology of post-traumatic stress disorder. *Psychiatric Clinics of North America.* 1998; 21:359-379.

78. Friedman MJ. Posttraumatic stress disorder. *Journal of Clinical Psychiatry.* 1997; 58(suppl 9):33-36.

79. Lovallo WR. *Stress and Health: Biological and Psychological Interactions. 2nd edition.* Thousand Oaks, CA: Sage Publications, 2005.

80. Flannery RB. *Post-Traumatic Stress Disorder.* New York: Crossroads, 1999.

81. Katz L, Fleisher W, Kjernisted K, Milanese P. A review of the psychobiology and pharmacotherapy of posttraumatic stress disorder. *Canadian Journal of Psychiatry.* 1996: 41:233-238.

82. Sutherland SM, Davidson JRT. Pharmacology for post-traumatic stress disorder. *Psychiatric Clinics of North America: Post-Traumatic Stress Disorder.* 1994; 17:409-423.

83. Friedman MJ. *Post Traumatic Stress Disorder.* Kansas City, MO: Compact Clinicals, 2001.

84. Nutt DJ. The psychobiology of posttraumatic stress disorder. *Journal of Clinical Psychiatry.* 2000; 61 (suppl 5):24-29.

85. Goldberg E. *The Executive Brain.* New York: Oxford University Press, 2001.

86. van der Kolk BA. The complexity of adaptation to trauma. In: van der Kolk BA, McFarlane AC, Weisaeth L, eds. *Traumatic Stress: The Effects of Overwhelming Experience on Mind, Body, and Society.* New York: Guilford Press, 1996:182-213.

87. McFarlane AC, Yehuda R, Clark RC. Biologic models of traumatic memories and post-traumatic stress disorder: The role of neural networks. *Psychiatric Clinics of North America.* 2002; 25:253-270.

88. Wright RJ, Finn P, Contreras JP, et al. Chronic caregiver stress and IgE expression, allergen-induced proliferation, and cytokine profiles in a birth cohort predisposed to atopy. *Journal of Allergy and Clinical Immunology.* 2004; 113:1051-1057.

89. Kiecolt-Glaser JK, Preacher KJ, MacCallum RC, Atkinson C, Malarkey WB, Glaser R. Chronic stress and age-related increases in the proinflammatory cytokine IL-6. *Proceedings of the National Academy of Sciences U.S.A.* 2003; 100:9090-9095.

90. Kiecolt-Glaser JK, McGuire L, Robles TF, Glaser R. Psychoneuroimmunology: psychological influences on immune function and health. *Journal of Consulting and Clinical Psychology.* 2002; 70:537-547.

91. Tillman RA. You and malpractice stress: II. One physician's story. *Journal of the Medical Association of Georgia.* 1986; 75:659.

92. Committee on Professional Liability. Coping with the stress of malpractice litigation. *International Journal of Gynaecology and Obstetrics.* 1995; 49:83-84.

93. Polles A, Neral S. The effects of malpractice on Mississippi physicians. *Journal of the Mississippi State Medical Association.* March 1993:77-81.

94. Charles SC. The physician and malpractice litigation. *Medical Practice Management.* 1985; 1:123-129.

95. Beck J. It's time to stand up for ourselves. *Journal of the Arkansas Medical Society.* 2004;101(5):135.

96. Shapiro RS, Simpson DE, Lawrence SL, Talsky AM, Sobosinski KA, Scheidermayer DL. A survey of sued and nonsued physicians and suing patients. *Archives of Internal Medicine.* 1989; 149:2190-2196.

97. Studdert DM, Mello MM, Sage WM, et al. Defensive medicine among high-risk specialist physicians in a volatile malpractice environment. *Journal of the American Medical Association.* 2005; 293(21):2609-2617.

98. Palmisano DJ. Health care in crisis: the need for medical liability reform. *Yale Journal of Health Policy, Law, and Ethics.* Winter 2005; 5(1):371-383.

99. Berenson RA, Kuo S, May JH. Medical malpractice liability crisis meets markets: stress in unexpected places. Center for Studying Health System Changes. 2003 September; Issue Brief No. 68. Available at: www.hschange.org/CONTENT/605/?words=malpractice. Accessed June 15, 2005.

100. Sheaffer M. Quoted in: Hoepfer M. Withstanding the stress of litigation. *Pennsylvania Medicine.* March *1997:22-24.*

101. Florida Academic Task Force for Review of the Insurance and Tort Systems, Preliminary Fact-Finding Report on Medical Malpractice. August 14, 1987: 244-254. In: Dewar MA, MacCrary SV, Allen WL. Medical malpractice. *American Family Physician.* 1993; 47: 1073-1074.

102. Glabman M. Specialist shortage shakes emergency rooms; more hospitals forced to pay for specialist care. *Physician Executive.* 2005; 31(3):6-11.

103. Reineck M. Handling malpractice stress: suggestions for physicians and their families. In: Bassett FH, ed. Instructional course lectures. *American Academy of Orthopaedic Surgeons.* 1988; 37:285.

104. Atkinson L, McBride D. Being sued: the loneliest feeling in the world. *Iowa Medicine.* January/February 1997:16-18.

105. Anonymous Member, Auxiliary to the MAG. A doctor's lawsuit – behind the scenes. *Journal of the Medical Association of Georgia.* 1986; 75:725.

106. Montgomery M. You and malpractice stress: III. Two spouses views. *Journal of the Medical Association of Georgia.* 1986; 75: 723-724.

107. Gardner ER, Hall RCW. Protracted stress syndrome in health care providers. *Texas Medicine.* 1980; 76:63-65.

108. Hutchison JR, Hutchison SA. The despair of liability litigation: a family affair. *Obstetrical and Gynecological Survey.* 2004; 59(9):641-642.

109. Shalev AY. Stress versus traumatic stress: From acute homeostatic reactions to chronic psychopathology. In: van der Kolk BA, McFarlane AC, Weisaeth L, eds. *Traumatic Stress: The Effects of Overwhelming Experience on Mind, Body, and Society.* New York: Guildford Press, 1996:77-101.

110. Brazeau CM. Coping with the stress of being sued. *Family Practice Management.* 2001; 8:41-44.

111. Charles SC. Coping with a medical malpractice suit. *Western Journal of Medicine.* 2001; 174:55-58.

112. American College of Obstetricians and Gynecologists, Department of Professional Liability. *Litigation Assistant: A Guide for the Defendant Physician. 2nd edition.* Washington, DC: American College of Obstetricians and Gynecologists, 1998.

113. Lobe TE. *Medical Malpractice: A Physician's Guide.* New York: McGraw-Hill, 1995.

114. Demos MP. What every physician should know about the National Practitioner Data Bank. *Archives of Internal Medicine.* 1991; 151:1708-1711.

115. Gray J. How did it ever come to this? *Medical Economics.* October 19, 1998:104-116.

116. Josefson D. Patients may gain access to doctors' disciplinary data. *Western Journal of Medicine.* 2000; 173:298-299.

117. Kohn LT, Corrigan JM, Donaldson MS, eds. *To Err Is Human: Building a Safer Health System.* Washington, DC: National Academy Press; 1999. Available at: http://www.nap.edu/html/to_err_is_human. Accessed January 18, 2003.

118. Goldberg RM, Kuhn G, Andrew LB, Thomas HA. Coping with medical mistakes and errors in judgment. *Annals of Emergency Medicine.* March 2002; 39(3):287-292. Available at: http://home.mdconsult.com/das/article/body/1/jorg=journal&source=&sp=12252596&s.../1.htm. Accessed July 24, 2002.

119. Mirvis DM. The other malpractice crisis: the link between malpractice liability and improved health care. *Tennessee Medicine.* May 2004:213-217.

120. Wu AW. Medical error: the second victim. *Western Journal of Medicine.* 2000; 172:358-359. EWJM. Available at: http://www.ewjm.com/cgi/content/full/172/6/358. Accessed December 8, 2002.

121. Christensen JF, Levinson W, Dunn PM. The heart of darkness: the impact of perceived mistakes on physicians. *Journal of General Internal Medicine.* 1992; 7:424-431.

122. Robinson AR, Hohmann KB, Rifkin JI, Topp D, Gilroy CM, Pickard JA, Anderson RJ. Physician and public opinions on quality of health care and the problem of medical errors. *Archives of Internal Medicine.* 2002; 162:2186-2190.

123. Tanner L. Doctors are urged to say they are sorry. Associated Press. November 11, 2004. Available at: http://ap.tbo.com/ap/breaking/MGBV71YEF1E.html. Accessed December 20, 2004.

124. Mazor KM, Simon SR, Gurwitz JH. Communicating with patients about medical errors: a review of the literature. *Archives of Internal Medicine.* 2004; 164:1690-1697.

125. Mazor KM, Simon SR, Yood RA, et al. Health plan members' views about disclosure of medical errors. *Annals of Internal Medicine.* 2004; 140:409-418.

126. Gallagher TH, Waterman AD, Ebers AG, Fraser VJ, Levinson W. Patients' and physicians' attitudes regarding the disclosure of medical errors. *Journal of the American Medical Association.* 2003; 289:1001-1007.

127. Why Sorry Works! works. Victims and Families United. Available at: www.victimsandfamilies.com/Sorry.phtml. Accessed December 20, 2004.

128. Zimmerman R. Doctors' new tool to fight lawsuits: saying "I'm sorry": malpractice insurers find owning up to errors soothes patient anger. *Journal of the Oklahoma Medical Association.* June 2004; 97(6):245-247.

129. Woods MS. *Healing Words: The Power of Apology in Medicine.* Oak Park, IL: Doctors in Touch, 2004.

130. Robeznieks A. The power of an apology: patients appreciate open communication. *Amednews.com,* July 28, 2003. Available at www.ama-assn.org/amednews/2003/07/28/prsa0728.htm. Accessed December 21, 2004.

131. Joint Commission on Accreditation of Healthcare Organizations. Sentinel event policy and procedures revised: July 2002. Available at www.jcaho.org/accredited+organizations/sentinel+event/se_pp.htm. Accessed December 12, 2004.

132. Gundersen L. Physician burnout. *Annals of Internal Medicine.* 2001; 135:145-148.

133. Gross CP, Mead LA, Ford DE, Klag MJ. Physician, heal thyself? Regular source of care and use of preventative health services among physicians. *Archives of Internal Medicine.* 2000; 160:3209-3214.

134. DeCaire MR, Alleman JM, Olbrich GD. A message from the Physicians Health Foundation of Louisiana. *Louisiana State Board of Medical Examiners Newsletter.* July 2003:1-2.

135. Baldessarini RJ. Drugs and the treatment of psychiatric disorders: depression and anxiety disorders. In: Hardman JG, Limbird LE, Gilman AG, eds. *Goodman and Gilman's The Pharmacological Basis of Therapeutics.* 10th edition. New York: McGraw Hill; 2001:447-478.

136. Restak R. *The Secret Life of the Brain.* Washington, DC: Joseph Henry Press, 2001.

137. Gage FH. Brain, repair yourself. *Scientific American.* Special Issue. September 2003:47-53.

138. Gorney M. Coping with bad news: the physician executive's role in a lawsuit. *Physician Executive.* March-April 2002:26-29.

139. Simon GE, Ludman EJ, Tutty S, Operskalski B, Von Korff M. Telephone psychotherapy and telephone care management for primary care patients starting antidepressant treatment. *Journal of the American Medical Association.* 2004; 292(8):935-942.

140. Schear W. Coping with the stress of malpractice litigation. *Connecticut Medicine.* October 1990:567-570.

141. Charles SC. How to handle the stress of litigation. *Clinics in Plastic Surgery.* 1999; 26:69-77.

142. Horan DW. Risk reduction from a plaintiff attorney's perspective. In: Anderson RE, ed. *Medical Malpractice: A Physician's Sourcebook.* Totowa, NJ: Humana Press, 2005:35-40.

143. Epstein JI. The judicial process: discovery and deposition. In: Anderson RE, ed. *Medical Malpractice: A Physician's Sourcebook.* Totowa, NJ: Humana Press, 2005:53-62.

144. United States Department of Health, Education, and Welfare. *Report of the Secretary's Commission on Medical Malpractice.* Washington, DC: DHEW Publication OS-73-78; 1973.

145. Pfifferling JH. Overcoming compassion fatigue. *Family Practice Management.* April 2000; 7(4). Available at: http://www.aafp.org/fpm/20000400/39over.html. Accessed January 18, 2003.

146. Spickard A, Gabbe SG, Christensen JF. Mid-career burnout in generalist and specialist physicians. *Journal of the American Medical Association.* 2002; 288(12):1447-1450.

147. Crane M. Why burned-out doctors get sued more often. *Medical Economics.* May 26, 1998:210-218.

148. Holthaus D. Reduce malpractice risks through better communication. *Hospitals.* November 20, 1987:50.

149. Passineau TL. Quoted in: Crane M. Why burned-out doctors get sued more often. *Medical Economics.* May 26, 1998:210-218.

150. Kabat-Zinn J. *Full Catastrophe Living: Using the Wisdom of Your Body and Mind to Face Stress, Pain and Illness.* New York: Delacorte Press, 1990.

151. Levini E. Mindfulness medication: modern medicine turns to an ancient practice. *abcnews.com,* July 5, 2002. Available at: http://abcnews.go.com/sections/living/DailyNews/mindfulness0705.html. Accessed January 18, 2003.

152. Millea PJ, Holloway RL. Use of mindfulness meditation for fibromyalgia. *American Family Physician.* 2002; 65:380,384. Available at: http://www.aafp.org/afp/20020201/letters.html. Accessed July 19, 2004.

153. Lutz A, Greischar LL, Rawlings NB, Matthieu R, Davidson RJ. Long-term meditators self-induce high-amplitude gamma synchrony during mental practice. *Proceedings of the National Academy of Sciences U.S.A.* 2004; 101(46):16369-16373.

154. Carlson LE, Ursuliak Z, Goodey E, Angen M, Speca M. The effects of a mindfulness meditation-based stress reduction program on mood and symptoms of stress in cancer outpatients: 6-month follow-up. *Support Care Cancer.* 2001; 9:112-123.

155. Kabat-Zinn J, Wheeler E, Light T, et al. Influence of a mindfulness meditation-based stress reduction intervention on rates of skin clearing in patients with moderate to severe psoriasis undergoing phototherapy (UVB) and photochemotherapy (PUVA). *Psychosomatic Medicine.* 1998; 60:625-632.

156. Kabat-Zinn J, Lipworth L, Burney R. The clinical use of mindfulness meditation for the self-regulation of chronic pain. *Journal of Behavioral Medicine.* 1985; 8:163-190.

157. Kaplan KH, Goldenberg DL, Galvin-Nadeau M. The impact of a meditation-based stress reduction program on fibromyalgia. *General Hospital Psychiatry.* 1993; 15:284-289.

158. Miller JJ, Fletcher K, Kabat-Zinn J. Three-year follow-up and clinical implications of a mindfulness meditation-based stress reduction intervention in the treatment of anxiety disorders. *General Hospital Psychiatry.* 1995; 17:192-200.

159. Dement W, Vaughan C. *The Promise of Sleep.* New York: Delacorte Press, 1999.

160. Mueller PS, Plevak DJ, Rummans TA. Religious involvement, spirituality, and medicine: implications for clinical practice. *Mayo Clinic Proceedings.* 2001; 76:1225-1235.

161. Frisch PR, Charles SC, Gibbons RD, Hedeker D. Role of previous claims and specialty on the effectiveness of risk-management education for office-based physicians. *Western Journal of Medicine.* 1995; 163:346-350.

162. Beckman HB, Markakis KM, Suchman AL, Frankel RM. The doctor-patient relationship and malpractice. *Archives of Internal Medicine.* 1994; 154:1365-1370.

163. Studdert DM, Mello MM, Brennan TA. Medical malpractice. *New England Journal of Medicine.* 2004; 350(3):283.

164. Levinson W, Roter DL, Mullooly JP, Dull VT, Frankel RM. Physician-patient communication: the relationship with malpractice claims among primary care physicians and surgeons. *Journal of the American Medical Association.* 1997; 277:553-559.

165. Ambady N, LaPlante D, Nguyen T, Rosenthal R, Chaumeton N, Levinson W. Surgeons' tone of voice: a clue to malpractice history. *Surgery.* 2002; 132:5-9.

166. Wissow LS. Communication and malpractice claims – where are we now? *Patient Education and Counseling.* 2004; 52:3-5.

167. Bell RA, Kravitz RL, Thom D, Krupat E, Azari R. Unsaid but not forgotten: patients' unvoiced desires in office visits. *Archives of Internal Medicine.* 2001; 161:1977-1984.

168. Horsley J. How to keep the patient's family from thinking "lawsuit." *Medical Economics.* February 4, 1991:146-149.

169. Kennedy R. Why patients become plaintiffs. *Letter of the Louisiana Medical Mutual Insurance Company.* 2001; 19:5-6.

170. May ML, Stengel DB. Who sues their doctor? How patients handle medical grievances. *Law and Society Review.* 1990; 24: 105-120.

171. Hickson GE, Clayton W, Entman SS, et al. Obstetricians' prior malpractice experience and patients' satisfaction with care. *Journal of the American Medical Association.* 1994; 272:1583-1587.

172. Adamson TE, Baldwin DC Jr, Sheehan TJ, Oppenberg AA. Characteristics of surgeons with high and low malpractice claims rates. *Western Journal of Medicine.* 1997; 166:37-44.

173. Weiner EL, Swain GR, Wolf B, Gottlieb M. A qualitative study of physicians' own wellness-promotion practices. *Western Journal of Medicine.* 2001; 174:19-23.

174. Smyth JM, Stone AA, Hurewitz A, Kaell A. Effects of writing about stressful experiences on symptom reduction in patients with asthma or rheumatoid arthritis. *Journal of the American Medical Association.* 1999; 281(14):1304-1309.

175. Stone AA, Smyth JM, Hurewitz A, Kaell A. Symptom reduction after writing about stressful experiences (Letter). *Journal of the American Medical Association.* 1999; 282:1811-1812.

176. Klapow J, Schmidt SM, Taylor LA, et al. Symptom management in older primary care patients: feasibility of an experimental, written self-disclosure protocol. *Annals of Internal Medicine.* 2001; 134:905-911.

177. Stanton AL, Danoff-Burg S, Sworowski LA, et al. Randomized, controlled trial of written emotional expression and benefit finding in breast cancer patients. *Journal of Clinical Oncology.* 2002; 20:4160-4168.

178. Greenberg MA, Stone AA. Emotional disclosure about trauma and its relation to health: effects of previous disclosure and trauma severity. *Journal of Personality and Social Psychology.* 1992; 63:75-84.

179. Pennebaker JW, Colder M, Sharp LK. Accelerating the coping process. *Journal of Personality and Social Psychology.* 1990; 58:528-537.

180. Pennebaker JW, Kiecolt-Glaser JK, Glaser R. Disclosure of traumas and immune function: health implications for psychotherapy. *Journal of Consulting and Clinical Psychology.* 1988; 56:239-245.

181. Spiegel D. Healing words: emotional expression and disease outcome. *Journal of the American Medical Association.* 1999; 281:1328-1329.

182. Rabow MW, McPhee SJ. Doctoring to heal: fostering well-being among physicians through personal reflection. *Western Journal of Medicine.* 2001; 174:66-69.

PERMISSIONS

Van der Kolk, BA,. *"The Psychobiology of Posttraumatic Stress Disorder," The Journal of Clinical Psychiatry.* Volume 58(suppl 9), 16-24, 1997. Copyright 1997, Physicians Postgraduate Press. Adapted/Reprinted by permission.

Diagnostic Criteria tables reprinted with permission from the *Diagnostic and Statistical Manual of Mental Disorders, Fourth Edition, Text Revision,* Copyright 2000. American Psychiatric Association

Index

INDEX

INDEX

R

S

INDEX

NOTES